From My Window

Especially for you!
Gordon Wagner
1990

by Gordon Wagner

Published by the
Flying -W- Publishing Co.
P.O.Box 3118 Courtenay, B.C. V9N 5N3

Printed by Kask Graphics Ltd., Campbell River, B.C.
Electronic Typesetting by J.P. Gordon - Island Microsystems
Edited by Jane Sellwood, Campbell River, B.C.

For Shirley and Keith
wherever you are

ACKNOWLEDGEMENTS

"The Little House", and three of the poems in *From My Window* appeared in The Courtenay Comox Valley Record. I thank the publication for permisssion to reprint them here.

Photos on pages 176, 182 and 184 are from *Writing the Natural Way* by Gabriele Lusser Rico, published by J.P. Tracher, Inc. Los Angeles, California.

I thank Sandy Heybroek for the permission to photograph her painting of the "The Little House".

My thanks to Tammy Pilon for her illustrations.

Contents

Preface 1

The Beginning
Spring in Comox Bay 3
The Beginning 5

Ancestors
William Faulkner 12
Sylvester Faulkner 18
Elderhostel 23
Edna Staebler 30

The Story 37
An 1849 Wedding 39

Family 65
Leaving Home 67
Letter to My Son 74
A New Leg 77
A Night in Jail 85

Survey Notes 91
Gilean's Channel Rock 94
The Telephone Line Surveyor 106
Levack's Narrow Mine 113
The Little House on the Dyke Road 115
June's November 122

School Days 125
Daylight on the Humber 127
Coed Bathrooms 129
Donna of Humber's Osler Hall 135
The Boss's Desk 140
Verbs 143
Airline Pickpocket 144

Contents

Modern Times 147
    Roy's Repair 149
    Airport Monster 156
    The Girl I Forgot to Save 161
    Boston's Canaghan Tunnel 164
    American Efficiency 166
    Debra 170

Poems 173
    New Teeth 175
    Homochronos 177
    Shirley Wagner 179
    Keith 181
    Glenda Bogen's Frog 183
    Glenda Bogen's Inner Ear 185
    Ode to a Secretary 187
    Jimmy Barry 189
    Lloyd Edwards 191
    V.O. Spring 193
    Let Us Live 195
    Time 197
    Ode to Sam Skinner 199

The Ending
    Comox Bay's October 201

    The Author 203

Me

Or I
Why am I me
Who cast the dice
To make me what I am
One in a million found a home
To nurture me from one to many
Now I tread my weary way
Through the tangles
Of living love
To eternity
Back to
Me

PREFACE

I'm a stubble jumper transplanted by World War II from the cold, dry plains of Saskatchewan to British Columbia's lush rain forest of the Comox Valley.

I remember the postman's mask during the 1917 flu epidemic, recall the armistice of World War I, saw Markinch's first "Tin Lizzie", heard Regina's CKCK (forty miles away) on the town's first radio, shed my shoes when the snow was gone, and waited an eternity for summer holidays and Christmas.

In the dirty thirties I mixed high school and college in the dust bowl and graduated to a $20-per-month (five cents an hour) farm job. I migrated to Sudbury's nickel mines and $5 a day, and chucked the mines for Airforce room, board, and clothes at $1.80 a day. The Service took me to twenty-one countries, introduced me to the haven of Canada's West Coast, found me a wife and brought us to Courtenay.

In '45 jobs were scarce in the Comox Valley. If I got to Sudbury by the 21st of December I'd get back my miner's job with eight years of seniority. If I caught Thursday's E. & N. out of Courtenay I'd arrive in time. But I needed my shoes repaired.

Those shoes and Jimmy Ashton, Courtenay's one-eared cobbler, kept me in Courtenay. Searle's Shoes closed on Wednesday, and Jimmy's shop was in the rear, so I used the back door. I told him of my intended trip to Sudbury, and he turned his good ear to me and in a Cockney accent said, "If you can make a living in Sudbury, you can make a living here. I came here forty years ago and this town's been good to me."

I unpacked my trunk and stayed in Courtenay. This town's been good to me.

I articled to Vilhelm Schjelderup, Courtenay's Land Surveyor, and got my commission. For thirty-five years I've surveyed the hills, the bush and swamps of the Comox Valley, parts of the West Coast from Nanaimo to Prince Rupert and from Powell River to Nootka Sound. I retired, cleared a swamp and farmed for five years. We sold the farm in '84.

My "pump" has lost its ability to keep my extremities warm, so instead of wearing gloves and extra socks, I escape Canada's cold weather and live in a R.V. park called Venture Out in sunny Arizona. There, four years ago, I attended Doris Hastings' creative writing classes. I felt stuffed with stories and yearned to write. But without her patience, calm persistance and encouragement, this book would never have been written.

In *From My Window* I've shared my experiences and bared my soul. I thank the people who helped and encouraged me: Ivy, my first editor and number one fan; Marguerite, my patient copy editor and mentor; Sophie, my enthusiastic reader; Doris, for my first story, "The Beginning"; and Jane, who edited the manuscript for publication, for believing.

SPRING ON COMOX BAY

It's Monday morning – a brand new week. I've been awake since four-thirty, trying to organize my day and the thoughts running through my mind. Phrases, sentences, words, similes and metaphors – trying to grab them, to store them safely in my memory. But I know as I struggle to recapture those thoughts, so great when conceived, they will appear hopelessly "blah" later on paper. I must learn to take a clipboard or a tape recorder to bed with me.

The picture in our kitchen window changes every day. Our clocks, now on daylight-saving time, usher in the dawn an hour later. As the day's first glimmer creeps across the cloudless sky, I busy myself brewing coffee, poaching eggs and charring brown bread toast. As I settle down to breakfast, I'm spellbound by the beauty of our precious bay.

3

The morning air is scrubbed crisp and clean by last night's storm. A soft sheen lights the slightly rippled water of the bay and a patina of fine silver forms intricate patterns on its silky surface. The mountains are silhouetted black against the cloudless sky, like an under-exposed black and white photo. From across the bay, the scattered street lights of Royston flicker like spluttering candles. Ducks doze peacefully on the quiet waters. The old rail fence zigzags out to meet its reflection in the mirror surface of the high tide. Goose Spit juts its long arm into the bay and floating logs speck the silver platter.

A rosy hue seeps across the bay. The fresh snow on the mountain tops is the first to capture the baby-pink announcement of the new-born sun. Magically the bay's gleaming silver is transformed into the colour of fine cranberry glass, its glowing pinkness revealing valleys in the mountains. The sleepy houses of Royston peek through the rosy mist. The whole bay throbs with shimmering redness that grows higher. Brighter. The bay, the mountains and the sky shout the glory of the new day. The music of the dawn rises in a crashing crescendo of colour — the climax of the sunrise.

Slowly the colours change. Now the snow and the mountain sides reflect the yellow rays of the new sun. A pair of golden windows dazzles from a Royston home. The sky turns to cobalt blue, and the rippled waters of the bay sparkle like dancing sapphires. The growing light reveals the naval barracks on the jutting Comox Spit. The rail fence casts long crooked shadows across the dew-drenched lawn. Its pile of leaves rust in the fresh light. Ducks scurry out to sea, pursued by a bald eagle gliding gracefully across the bay. A fish boat slips around the spit, sailing into the rising sun.

My coffee's cold. The day's awake. It's time to go.

THE BEGINNING

For the third time Doris Hastings shuffled the pile of books, papers and files she had collected over the past thirty years. She looked despairingly at the disarray. Three times she reduced its size, but it would still take up too much space in the Oldsmobile. "Do I really need all this? Do I need any of it?"

She recognized an old notebook protruding from one of the stacks. It was the one she'd used in the first English course she'd taken from Professor Franklin. She eased it from its hiding place and ran her hand slowly over the cover.

Almost reverently she opened the loose-leaf notebook. Her eyes dropped to the notation in the margin. There in his familiar handwriting was Professor Franklin's "Good!". It had been her first assignment. She had written and rewritten that story a dozen times — the story of her father's struggle to wrest a farm from the wilds of Wisconsin and his marriage to her school-teacher mother. As she lingered over the lines, a warm nostalgia flooded her soul, brought a smile to her face and a misty dimness to her eyes.

Reluctantly she replaced the notebook. She wouldn't need it at Venture Out.

The idea of teaching a class in creative writing in that winter community of thirty-five hundred people intrigued her. All those people with all those years, must have hundreds of stories to tell. After years of retirement she looked forward to the stimulating challenge of a new class of students. She felt confident that Venture Out's vigorous "geritol" citizens would provide an interesting class.

She squeezed the last file, the last book and the last notebook into the cardboard box — all the space they could spare in the trunk of the car. She returned the others to their boxes and stored them in the attic.

Today was the day. Venture Out's recreational director had allotted her a classroom. Venture Outlines had announced her course in creative writing, but the telephone had not been busy. She'd get to class early as had been her custom for years. She'd put introductory suggestions on the blackboard, and be calmly settled when her first students arrived.

She paused for a moment as she gave a few finishing touches to her make-up. It had been quite a while since she'd retired from teaching advanced composition in California. She'd always been a bit nervous meeting a new class and felt a small knot in her stomach. But it was great to be active again. She knew she'd enjoy it and was anxious to get started.

The students came, a dozen or so — more than she expected. It amazed her how much a group of seniors resembled a class of teen-agers. They were all there: the front seaters and the back row talkers; the finger snappers (with the first answer, right or wrong, it didn't matter); the teacher's pet, and even Peck's bad boy. She soon settled down to her familiar classroom routine, and by the time she had them fill out their registration cards, the knot in her stomach untied and she began her first lesson.

The course was eight weeks old now, with one more class to go. The attendance had dropped slightly, and though these "geritolites" were not striving for credits, the assignments came in. They kept her busier than she'd anticipated, but she enjoyed it. She hoped they had and that they'd all be back next year.

In the fall of '86 I enrolled in the North Island College's English 120 with thirty-six high school grads and three housewives. I enjoyed Reg Garnett and the short stories and novels we studied in his class. In my first assignment I had to tell why I was taking the course, and I wrote:

> I've lived for seventy-two years and only used ten percent of the furrows convoluting my brain. Why not plough some new ones and clean out the old?

For the past six years I have been tracing the roots of my family. My genealogy indexes fifteen hundred people, tracing ancestors back to the late 1400s.

Jacob Wagner was a captain in Napoleon's bodyguard. He went with him to Moscow and froze and lost his toes in the retreat, but lived to tell how the last things to be abandoned were the carts of gold used to pay the soldiers. His son, my great-great-grandfather, settled near Rochester, N.Y. I found his farm and distant cousins living nearby.

Faulkner is my mother's family name. Edmund arrived in Andover, Massachusetts in 1635. I've found his farm. He was Andover's first town clerk. I have photocopies of the town meeting minutes he wrote three hundred years ago.

Andrew Kimmerly, another ancestor, joined the Royal New York Regiment when he was sixteen. The American Rebels chased him, along with General Johnston and the Iroquois warrior Joseph Brant, out of the Mohawk Valley. Andrew settled near the Bay of Quinte. He married Susannah Sager and had sixteen children. Napanee, Ontario crawls with Kimmerlys.

A thousand stories twirl through my mind. English 120 will help me pluck those tales from the furrows, plant people and places on printed pages, bring life to Andrew, to Jacob, and to Edmund. I will retrace the paths they trod, and take my readers with me.

From My Window

Ancestors

Wagner Family about 1900, Berlin, Ontario
Sarah (Moyer), Ida, Florence, Louis (Author's father),
Carl and Rev. Henry Wagner

William Faulkner

Gilbert Faulkner, grandfather of author

WILLIAM FAULKNER

For years the genealogy of my family has fascinated me, its wide-spreading branches leading my curious mind to speculate about the past. The more family history I find, the stronger the tie becomes between me and my ancestors. I find myself dreaming about them. Have I lived before? Do the spirits of my ancestors survive within me? My roots lead to four families, the Wagners, the Staeblers, the Blairs and the Faulkners.

Something began to happen. In the fall of 1982 and again in 1983, I found the homes of my mother's ancestors in Hastings County near Belleville Ontario. I drove along country roads, walked down shady lanes. Strangers welcomed me into their homes. I met a cousin who looked like my brother.

After an hour in Glen and Shirley Copley's farm kitchen, I felt I'd known them all my life. They were kinfolk. I had come home.

In the fall of 1984, I visited my eighty-year-old aunt in Regina. Elsie Faulkner's crisp memory drew vivid pictures of her early days with my mother. She told me the history of my own childhood. We touched on genealogy. "Gordon," she said, "I've always felt we're related to the author, William Faulkner, and I'll show you why." She disappeared for a moment.

I'd traced the Faulkners, who arrived in Massachuetts in 1635, back to Edmund, but I'd found no mention of the author. *We all like to think we're descended from the nobility — why not a famous writer? Humour her, Gordon!*

"Who does that look like?" Aunt Elsie demanded, as she handed me a copy of *Time*.

"That's Grandpa Faulkner!" I immediately recognized the pen-and-ink sketch on the cover. The triangular shape of the face, the sweep of the hair, the swirl of the mustache and the droop of the eyelids were copied from the face of her father,

Gilbert Faulkner, my grandfather.

The magazine was dated 17 July 1964, and featured an article about "William Faulkner". The Civil Rights Act of 1964 had just lived through its first week and Time reporter Horace Justin had used William Faulkner's story to take an in-depth look at the soul of the south and the problems it faced.

Sarah (Blair) Faulkner.

"Look," I gasped, "the right eyelid droops more than the left, just like mine." Aunt Elsie gave me the magazine and I carefully placed it with the other notes I had made of my visit.

When I returned home I started a course in creative writing, and our first assignment was to tell why we wanted to become writers. I wrote the following:

The showers of late September had surrendered to the warmth of the autumn sun as it began its descent. The chain-locked gate that guarded the East 1/2 of Lot

3, Section 8, Sidney Township, Hastings County, was framed by twin maples, beautiful in their autumn colours. Droplets of warm rain still clung to the fence wire and the colourful foliage, sparkled like rhinestones in the shadow — lengthening sun. It was good to let the beauty of the moment soak into my soul, good to be close to the home of the first Faulkner to settle in Canada, and good to feel that Sylvester Faulkner, my great — great — grandfather, had once stood on this very ground.

Sylvester Faulkner pre-empted the land in 1790. He, his wife Mary (nee Cram) and two of their children had emigrated from Sturbridge, Massachusetts after the war against the rebels. Their farm was about ten miles north of Belleville, Ontario, in an area known as the Faulkner settlement.

I had visited the farm the previous autumn, in search of some of my mother's ancestors. I had found Harry Faulkner, (a cousin several times removed) who owned the land that Sylvester Faulkner had home-steaded. The farm had become too much for Harry to manage, so he boarded up the buildings, padlocked the gate and moved to Belleville.

I climbed over the gate and started down the gravel driveway that led to the old house and barn, a quarter of a mile from the concession road. As I walked along the road, bordered on one side by hay fields and on the other by the neighbour's fence, the sky slowly darkened. I turned to see if a thunder cloud had covered the sun. The gravel road behind me had disappeared, and in its place a deer trail wandered through the moss-covered floor of the virgin forest. Giant maples, towering beeches and sturdy oaks hid the sinking sun. I turned. The hayfield was now part of the dense forest. The neighbour's fence had disappeared.

To my right I recognized the blazes that marked the

surveyed boundary of the lot. Following the blazes, I came upon a small clearing. In the middle of the clearing, surrounded by newly-felled trees, a spring gurgled. Then, from behind a huge maple a man emerged. He knelt by the spring, dipped his cupped hands in the cool water, and noisily slurped and splashed the water over his face.

I tripped and fell. "Damn that barbed wire." When I looked up, Sylvester's old house stood just as I had seen it the year before, and I could hear the gurgle of the spring.

How I wish I had had time to talk to the man by the spring. I'm sure it was Sylvester Faulkner.

In late November of 1984 we escaped the cold of British Columbia to enjoy the winter sun of Arizona. On my first visit to the Mesa Library, I found the books of William Faulkner.

Faulkner was a stranger. I had never read his books. From his twenty or more books I pulled *Sanctuary* from the shelf, and read the first paragraph: "From beyond the screen of the bushes which surrounded the spring, Popeye watched the man drinking. A faint path led from the road to the spring. Popeye watched the man — a tall thin man, hatless, in worn gray flannel trousers and carrying a tweed coat over his arm — emerge from the path and kneel to drink from the spring."

Excitement rose from some deep well within me. It was happening again! Was I a kinsman of William Faulkner? Or was he a genetic echo of myself? I was sure old Sylvester Faulkner had been there when I walked up the gravel road to his spring. Now here was William Faulkner.

I must find out more, get to know him. I read on: "The spring welled up at the root of the beech tree and flowed away upon a bottom of whorled and waved sand. It was surrounded by a thick growth of cane and briar, of cypress and gum in which broken sunlight lay sourceless. Somewhere, hidden and secret yet nearby, a bird sang three notes and ceased."

His words goosepimpled my mind. The spring danced through my own images of greenery and I heard the bird cease.

I plunged on, eager to see what I could find to link me to this new Faulkner. I skimmed through *Sanctuary*, decided to read it, and found a book on the life of William Faulkner. I borrowed both.

Walking home with Faulkner tucked protectively under my arm, my mind reeled as I contemplated a new adventure with the Faulkner family.

I stopped at the Mesa Genealogical Library. *Time* said that Faulkner was proud of his southern heritage and had lived most of his life in Oxford, Mississippi. I pulled the genealogical microfiche for Mississippi and then for the adjoining states of Tennessee and Arkansas. There were Faulkners, but none led to William. I stared at the names on the screen, wondering where to look next. I had discovered hundreds of Faulkners in New England, and at Andover, Massachusetts, and had verified Edmund's arrival in America. Given time, I would find William's forefathers.

But why should I see a man at the spring and find William Faulkner with a "man at the spring"? Why should I see Sylvester's farm the way it was in 1800? I knew I carried the same genes as Sylvester. Did William share these genes? I had to know.

I hurried home. My wife read the first paragraph of *Sanctuary* and gasped, "Gordon this is almost weird!"

"It's amazing! I couldn't find anything in the International Genealogical Index at the Mormon library. I must read *Time* again. Maybe my theory about gene reversal isn't as wild as we thought."

We know the DNA molecules in our genes carry our inherited characteristics from generation to generation, making William Faulkner look like my grandfather and my brother like cousin Harry and Sylvester. People with common genes would react to a given stimulus in a similar manner. Is this why I felt I had been on Sylvester's farm before?

Is this why we feel at home in strange places? Do I carry the same genes responsible for the words of William Faulkner? Could the phenomenon I experienced be my DNA working in reverse? Instead of the genes bringing the physical forward, couldn't they take thoughts or mental processes back? Did this account for the supernatural ordeal associated with reincarnation? My skepticism warned me to be careful.

I followed Popeye's ruthless life through *Sanctuary*, and lived through *Sartoris* with Faulkner's grandfather. I found Faulkner difficult to read but enjoyed the deep furrows he plowed across my mind, revelled in his use of words, let his images merge into my soul.

As an exercise in writing the natural way and using recurrence, I used the line "I'll never live long enough". Weeks later I reread the *Time* article about William Faulkner: Halfway through the writing of his third novel *Sartoris*, he had a vision: "I discovered that my own little postage stamp of native soil was worth writing about and that *I would never live long enough* to exhaust it. I created a cosmos of my own."

Was there no end to the Faulkner fantasy? William Faulkner was nearly a generation older than I. He died in 1962 at the age of sixty-five. In Oxford, Mississippi, the home of "Old Miss", the university has a Faulkner collection. I wrote to their librarian, hoping to find more about this Nobel Prize winning author.

On the shelf of a second-hand book store, I found four of Faulkner's books. I will take him back to Canada, keep him near me, read him with tender loving care. I may not live long enough to write like William Faulkner, but I will write.

SYLVESTER FAULKNER

I untangled myself from the grasping barb wire and walked slowly to Sylvester Faulkner's house, well aware of the hallucination I had experienced on the graveled driveway. I approached the house with reverence, as though I were entering a shrine. Perhaps I was gifted with the ability to communicate with the past.

I wanted desperately to take something with me when I left Sylvester's farm, something Sylvester had made that I could keep near me, see it often, touch it, and let it become a part of me. Perhaps I could capture it in a painting or a sketch. A strong, urgent need gripped me.

Cousin Harry had pointed out the old porch guarding the back door. The time-stained porch was older than the rest of the house and the porch door even older. Sylvester had handcrafted the door almost two hundred years ago, and it still functioned. I lifted the aged latch and opened the door. A network of cobwebs draped the entrance. I brushed them aside and reached for the white enameled door knob hanging loosely on the pale green door. The door creaked open to reveal a large farm kitchen. A narrow window caught the dwindling light of the late afternoon. I looked for a light switch to chase the gloom from the room. A single cord dangled a light bulb from the nine-foot ceiling. I clicked the old fashioned side-switch three times. There was no power.

Under the fly-specked window stood a long kitchen table covered with a sagging piece of oilcloth. Two chairs anchored the ends of the table, and a long well-used bench guarded the side. Against the wall opposite the window sat a squat kitchen stove with a hot-water reservoir. A large woodbox fitted neatly between the reservoir and the wall. Beside the stove sat a ladder-back rocking chair with a rush-bottom seat.

Two pale green doors with white enameled door knobs led from the room. One, to the left of the stove, concealed a pantry and a steep stairway; the other, opposite the entrance, took me into the abandoned parlor. The pattern on the linoleum struggled with worn-out brown areas and a thick blanket of dust. An old, over-stuffed armchair, askew on three legs, leaned against a broken window. Lace curtains had flung their tattered ends across the back of the chair. A second window, draped with a tired green blind, looked out onto the veranda. The door to the veranda was locked. Stove pipes kinked a connection between a rusting Quebec heater and a bracketed chimney. Over the heater a grating gaped to the room upstairs. Over the musty smell of the stuffy room I caught the odour of tobacco smoke. It seemed to be coming from the kitchen.

As I stepped back into the kitchen and closed the door, a sudden brightness flooded the room. I glanced up at the light bulb and then to the window. The sinking sun had found its way through the clouds and past the huge maple protecting the window. It shone into the room. I could feel the warmth. Slowly a comforting coziness filled the old kitchen.

Surely that warmth isn't coming from the sun, I thought. *It must be from the stove.*

I heard a creak. Was that the rocking chair? Had there been a small earthquake?

I smelled smoke — tobacco smoke.

I shivered. Could it be happening to me again? Heat was coming from the stove. The rocking chair had the creaking rhythm of occupancy, and the smoke was coming from a well-used pipe. I recognized the man in the rocking chair immediately.

"Carl!" I gasped, "What are you doing here, and where did you get that homespun outfit?"

"Nope. Not Carl," said the squat, heavy-set man as he rose from the rocker, "I'm Sylvester Faulkner."

"I'm Gordon Wagner," I stammered, as I felt the warm, firm grip of his well-callused hand.

"You must be my great-great-grandfather!" I felt a kindred sensation tingle through our clasped hands. We shared the same genes — no wonder he looked like my brother Carl.

"Pull up a chair and sit down," he said, settling into the rocking chair. "I've been watching you this past year, ever since Harry showed you the farm. Inquisitive, aren't you? Taking those new-fangled tintypes of the farm, the church and the graveyard with your new-fangled camera. I'm happy to know you're interested in the family." He paused to tamp his pipe.

"I've been watching this place for nigh unto two hundred years. Whole countryside used to be full of Faulkners and their kinfolk. Still lots of them around, but family doesn't seem to be important anymore. Harry and his father Gilbert kept the farm going for the past fifty years. The place is looking tired and run down. Don't know what'll happen now, Harry being a bachelor. I suppose the place will pass out of the family. If it does I'll have to leave — couldn't stand strangers around."

"I've been tracing my family roots these past few years," I said. "That's how I found your place. I was hoping that you might be able to help me."

"Be glad to do what I can. You're the great grandson of my boy, Francis Dwight. You found his place top the hill a mile west of here. Good farmer living there now — but not a Faulkner. All of Dwight's boys went to the northwest in the eighties, all four of them."

"That's right. I'm the grandson of his son Gilbert. I've been using the records of the Mormon Church, and I think I've traced the Faulkners back to England."

"That's where we came from. I mind my grandfather Daniel's family Bible. Mary and I had one, but it got burned in a fire when we lived in Lancaster, Massachuetts. I don't take to you keeping company with those Mormons. Angels of Satan they are! Why I hear that at one time you thought that your great-grandmother had been born out of wedlock. Gordon, things like that just don't happen in Baptist families. We Faulkners are God-fearing people. Always have been. Why, I built the first church at the crossroads. Built the manse too. It's still standing. Bunch of queer people living in it now. Hippies, they call them." To emphasize his disgust, he opened the fire box and spat angrily into the glowing coals.

Dare I ask more? He was obviously upset, but I was anxious to take advantage of this new source of information, so I blundered on, telling him what I knew.

Sylvester's son, Francis Dwight, had married Ellen Kimmerly, the daughter of Andrew Kimmerly and Huldah Ostrom. I had a copy of Andrew Kimmerly's will. He died in 1828. Ellen, her mother Huldah and her two brothers, George and Allen, were beneficiaries.

Lottie (Faulkner) Fuller, my mother's cousin and the family historian, showed that Ellen had been born on 11 July 1821. This date agreed with the *Belleville Intelligencer* article reporting her death on 29 May 1896, in her seventy-sixth year. Records on file in the Belleville Public Library showed that her parents, Andrew

and Huldah, had been married on 14 May 1822, by Reverend Mc-
Dowell of Kingston, Ontario.

I had confirmed this in the archives of the United Church in
Toronto.

Sylvester listened patiently as I told my story, his shaggy
eyebrows frowning over his deep set eyes. I could feel them
boring through me. The rocker had stopped. He stood up and
slowly and deliberately added wood to the fire.

He settled back in his rocker. "You're right about the dates,
and that happened quite often. In those early days Reverend Mc-
Dowell was the only ordained minister between Kingston and
Lake Huron. Used to come through once a year, and if you missed
him you'd have to wait until his next trip. The Kimmerlys were
Lutheran, had a church at Big Creek, usually had a lay preacher.
Andrew and Ellen must have been married there, then had a
proper service the first time Reverend McDowell came by. That
sort of thing happened all the time, same with christenings."

"I suspected that might be the explanation. At one time I
thought Ellen might be the sixteenth child of Andrew Kimmerly
and Susannah Sager. The dates seemed to indicate that."

"No, she was the daughter of his son Andrew. Young
Andrew, they called him — a real scalawag. If he hadn't died so
young, could have owned half of Belleville. Had a whiskey still.
Got to drinking his own liquor and died before he was thirty. We
weren't too happy when Francis married Ellen. Never could
stand those Dutchmen — especially young Andrew. Why in 1813,
during the war against the Yankees, they say he leased his sloop,
the Betsy, to the British and then helped the Yankees sink her.
Collected the rent and the insurance, too. But Ellen was a mighty
fine girl — good wife — great mother. Took after my Mary, God
bless her."

A wave of compassion flooded through me as I studied his
sad face. A tear gathered in the corner of his eyes and trickled
down his wrinkled cheek. "How old are you?" I asked.

"Same age as you," he snapped. "Be seventy-one next spring.

Been mighty lonely around here since Mary died."

Suddenly the room darkened. I looked up at the dangling unlit light bulb, and glanced at the window. A deep twilight had settled over the farm. An eerie chill passed through the room. I shivered. The rocking chair was empty. I thought I saw it move ever so slightly. I put my hand on the stove. It was cold. It was time to go.

I walked down the graveled road, and climbed over the chain-locked gate. I paused, rested my arms on top of the gate, and gazed back at the hayfield and the road. In the soft moonlight of the quiet evening a wave of warmth flooded my soul.

I sighed contentedly as I got into my rented car and headed down the Baptist Church Road to Belleville, taking with me another treasure of the Faulkner family.

ELDERHOSTEL

Did you ever find the end of a rainbow? I did. I found mine in North Andover, in the state of Massachusetts. Elderhostel took me to North Andover's Merrimack College. There, I found my pot of gold and brought it home back to Comox, on British Columbia's Vancouver Island.

The Elderhostel program is designed to make year-round use of universities and colleges by offering courses to senior citizens. If you are over sixty, you can go back to school at colleges all over the world. Courses last a week. Three subjects are offered and you may take one, two or three. You live in the student dormitories, eat in the cafeteria and use all the facilities of the campus. You must get yourself to and from the college. The fee for the three courses is $205, which includes your room and board.

I'd traced my mother's family back to Edmund, the first Faulkner to come to America. Edmund arrived from England in 1635 and was one of Andover's first settlers. In 1759 Daniel Faulkner married Sarah Shumway; the Shumway's town was Oxford just twenty miles away. Salem State and Andover's

Merrimack College had courses in July. I called the Boston office of the Elderhostel and was accepted by both colleges.

How lucky can you get! The three towns are within a radius of twenty-five miles, thirty-five miles north-west of Boston. Classes were from 9 a.m. to 2:30 p.m. I'd have plenty of time to find Edmund Faulkner's land and look for Shumway's too.

As a land surveyor, I have found four of the farms settled by my ancestors. I found the land in Lyons, N.Y. (near Rochester) where the Wagners lived when they came from Germany in 1830. I found Sylvester Faulkner's farm north of Belleville, Ontario. He came to the Bay of Quinte in 1790 to escape the harassment of the American Rebels. It's still in the family, and farmed by a distant cousin, Harry Faulkner.

I traced the military career of Andrew Kimmerly. During the American Revolution he was in the Royal New York Regiment and fled from upper New York State's Mohawk Valley. As an Empire Loyalist he got 200 acres near Napanee, Ontario, and because he fought the American Rebels, he got an extra 200 acres, and each of his sixteen children got 50 acres.

I followed Jacob Hailer through his apprenticeship as a wheelwright in the Duchy of Baden in Germany, to his voyage to America. His 92-day crossing was twenty days longer than Colombus's voyage to the New World. Aboard ship he met and married Margaret Riehl. They barged up the Erie Canal to Buffalo. He entered Canada at Fort Erie, then went to Berlin (Kitchener) Ontario, where in 1832 they built a home and woodworking shop. I found the lot on King St. near Kitchener's Farmers' Market.

I had brought a piece of the land (a small rock) from the first four farms I had found. Now I needed a stone from Andover.

I flew from Comox to Toronto, rented a car and drove to Salem, Massachuetts.

Americans are proud of their educational institutions. The routes to all their colleges are well marked. I found the campus of Salem State and walked into the lobby of Peabody Hall.

24

"You must be Gordon Wagner. Welcome to Elderhostel and Salem State. I'm Nancy Bodenstein." She offered me her hand. She glowed "Welcome". A quiet beauty smiled from her classic oval face. With her hair combed straight back, she radiated friendliness. "I'll be looking after you people for the next week. This is Marie. She and Paul will see you get a room and help you with your luggage."

"I'm beginning to like it already. I had a long drive today." I moved to the registration desks. "You're Marie? Do you have anything left?" I kidded. "I'd like a quiet room, away from the traffic."

"I'm sorry Mr. Wagner, but I don't have a room for you. I'm going to have to put you on the second floor with the married couples. You'll have to use the bathroom and showers on the third floor." She was dark, real dark, and warm and friendly. "Here's your key. You're in room 320, right next door to Paul. He'll help you with your bags. I'll get some linen, towels and a pillow for you."

Paul helped me with my luggage and showed me the men's showers and wash room, the study and the common room with its black and white TV, fridge and kitchen stove.

My room reminded me of the bunkhouses I'd lived in, with concrete-brick walls decorated with student graffiti. A large window centred the outside wall overlooking a playground of the housing compound, and peeked through the sycamore trees at Salem's harbour. Iron-framed cots huddled into their corners, and a pair of desks faced each other and shared the window. On the hall wall a chest of drawers guarded both sides of the door. Three by three wardrobes tried to fill the corners and hide your clothes behind flimsy vinyl doors.

Marie arrived. "Here's your sheets, blankets and towels, and if there is anything you need, my room is at the end of the hall. We want you to be comfortable."

"What time is dinner?" I asked.

"We'll meet in the main lounge in forty-five minutes and we'll lead you to the cafeteria. 'Bye, Mr. Wagner. See you later."

So this would be home for the next week. It was clean and adequate. I was tired after the long drive. I kicked off my boots, pillow-slipped my pillow, doubled it under my head and stretched out on the bare mattress.

It had been fifty years since I had been to college. There were thirty-nine people in our class. They were no different than those of fifty years ago.

There were the front seaters (I was one now because I couldn't hear well); a couple of finger snappers who, right or wrong always had an answer; teacher's pets, who always had their assignments done, and a little more besides; those who were against everything and enjoyed being cantankerous; a meek one whose knowledge, wit and humor amazed us when it emerged from behind a quiet face; and one or two who thought they should be teaching the class but stumbled early.

Professor John Fox, a fiery Irish New Englander, gave a great class in genealogy with special attention to Oral History. In photography, Professor Bantly took us on a field trip, gave each of us a roll of film and provided cameras. Effective Writing's Professor Kessler made us write, and that is always good. Most of us were too damned wordy. But he was patient and we learned to listen and tolerate ourselves as well as others.

After classes, eager to find more about the Faulkners, I searched the Land Title Office, the municipal offices, libraries, museums and historical societies.

Dr. Nancy Bodenstein and her staff made it a week of joy. Friday, our last day together, we had a cook-out. All the staff and their spouses attended. They fed us barbecued chicken, burgers, fresh corn and strawberry short cake, and presented us with a graduation certificate. We responded with our yell.

SALEM SALEM ELDERHOST
WE'RE THE BEST YOU'RE THE BOSS
SALEM SALEM RAH RAH RAH

"An Elderhostel first!" Dr. Nancy claimed.

The second week I moved to Merrimack College in Andover, a young college (1947) with a beautiful campus. I had an apartment designed for four students, with two bedrooms, two bathrooms, a sitting room and a fully modern kitchen. A new caterer fed us food too good not to eat. My belly bulged.

Dr. Ann Arsenault introduced us to their fine campus. We studied New England writers, Hawthorne with Dr. Kathy Cain, and Thoreau with Dr. Elaine Huber. The class visited Walden Pond. Dr. Carrie Poirier's class, "Mill Towns of New England", presented with excellent lectures and tours, opened a new world of New England's industrial and social history.

But I'd come a long way to find more about Edmund Faulkner. Being a teacher's pet, I got permission to skip classes to continue my research. I was beginning to despair when Wednesday morning at breakfast a woman classmate said, "We found Edmund Faulkner's gravestone yesterday."

I choked. "Where?" I asked.

"In the Old Cemetery. It's not far. We could go before our 8:30 class."

It was the grave of Edmund Faulkner. He died on the 18th of January, 1687. His son Francis is buried beside him.

I was getting closer. As I drove the roads of Andover, I had the feeling I'd been here before, the feeling I had on Sylvester Faulkner's farm in Foxborough, Ontario.

Then I found my rainbow. It's strange how things happen. I asked to be excused from a class tour of Dr. Poirier's Mill Towns course, telling her about my search for the Faulkners.

"You shouldn't miss today's tour. Any but today's."

"I've come 3000 miles. My time is getting short," I said.

"If you come, I'll bring you my copy of *Four Generations of Andover*. It's a recent publication and is bound to have something about the Faulkners."

The tour was good. Lowell, the mill town, was named after the Boston Lowells, who spoke only to the Cabots. The Cabots spoke only to God.

The book helped. A foot-note thanked Forbes Rockwell for the use of his early maps of Andover. "Do you know Forbes Rockwell?" I asked the woman who'd found Edmund's grave.

"His cousin Bob is the College librarian," she replied.

I got Forbes Rockwell's number from his cousin. A woman with a southern accent answered and I told her who I was and why I wanted Forbes. The phone dripped mint-julep honey. "If that's what you're all doing, Forbes will just **love** to see you."

Half an hour later I was in Forbes Rockwell's 250-year-old house. His third-floor study overflowed with filing cabinets, a computer, shelves of books and piles of paper. *This is your man, Gordon. How the hell can you get this lucky? Are you being led around or pushed by a guiding force? Or maybe your persistence is paying off. Never mind Gordon, take it.*

Edmund Faulkner had been Andover's first town clerk. The

28

minutes of the earliest meetings are in his handwriting. In 1961 the 300-year-old minutes had been microfilmed, deciphered and indexed. Forbes Rockwell had been the editor. Forbes was an engineer and a surveyor. The selectmen of the town divided and allotted land as new settlers came and families grew. He'd plotted their weird descriptions, had them on maps. "Do you know where the original Faulkner lived?" I asked.

"Yes. I just finished doing a resume for the Holt family. Their land was near Edmund Faulkner's. I've got a map here somewhere. Here it is. Faulkner's was one lot from the corner. I'll show it to you."

"I can't tell you what this means to me. It all seems like a dream. Like the pot of gold at end of the rainbow."

As we left the house I noticed two large oil portraits, a man and a woman. "Your ancestors?" I asked.

"Yes. The man's a Rockwell. She's a Shumway."

"Shumway! I've Shumways in the family. Daniel Faulkner married a Sarah Shumway. All the Shumways in America are said to be descended from the French Hugenot who settled in Oxford Massachusetts, in 1695."

We discovered we were distant cousins.

He took me to the ground Edmund Faulkner tilled so many years ago. North Andover's Kittredge School guards the land today. I dug a rock from beneath the grassy field.

I got it home and cleaned it. It dazzled me with gold, fool's gold and bits of flashing mica. It glittered in our British Columbia sunshine. And why not? It had come from the foot of an Andover rainbow Forbes Rockwell and Elderhostel had helped me find.

EDNA STAEBLER

She's famous, and I'm not used to famous people. We have her cookbook—*Food that Really Schmeks*—and I've seen her on TV. She was on "The Fifth Estate" about the Cookie War, and I read her cookie war story in *Saturday Night*. I found one of her stories in Air Canada's *Enroute*, hidden in the seat-back pocket with the safety instructions and sick bag. You don't get featured in *Saturday Night*, or travel with *Enroute* unless you write well. Really well!

"Edna Staebler's Sun Fish Lake"

I'd just written a story of the courtship and marriage of my great grandparents. In 1849, Jacob Wagner of Albany, New York, wrote to the Jacob Hailers, of Berlin, Upper Canada, (now Kitchener, Ontario) asking consent to marry their daughter Margaret. I have the letter and the envelope—they wear their one hundred forty years well. The firm German script marches across the page with military precision, demanding to be read at attention.

Now my wife and other encouraging critics wanted the next chapter, so I had to know more about those ancestors. I had to travel the roads they traveled, seek out their farms, get my hands into the soil they tilled, talk to friends, distant cousins and strangers. I knew Edna Staebler lived in the Kitchener area.

I had to go to Kitchener ...

The area retains much of its German-Mennonite culture, and Edna Staebler knows their traditions, has lived amongst them and written about them and their recipes. Besides, we were related by marriage. Her former husband was my second cousin, and judging from the way she wrote, she'd be strong on family. I wondered if she'd see me. I could phone and ask.

I'm shy on the telephone, but information gave me a number for an E. Staebler with a rural address. I'd call her – but first, I'd read her *Saturday Night* story again, check her cookbook and review the Staebler genealogy.

The number rang several times. Maybe she wasn't home. Then a sleepy voice said, "Hello?" I had *Edna Staebler* on the line!

I told her who I was, what I was doing and asked if I could see her. As we talked I forgot my shyness, for her 'phonogenic' voice glowed with enthusiasm. "I'll be happy to see you. Call me when you get to Toronto." A week later the same smiling voice directed me to her place on Sunfish Lake.

I took a wrong turn off 401, but a friendly farmer put me back on course. I twisted along the graveled backroads of Waterloo County to a rail fence circling the end of the road and guarding (from a safe distance), a tree-trunk coloured cottage. Signs on the fence said "Hodson" and "Beware of Dog". I left my briefcase in the car, wary of "Hodson & Dog."

From a gap in the fence a newly-laid concrete block walk crying for moss and age led straight to the back door. The weathered cedar cottage and the tree trunks still wore their winter clothes, providing a soft, sooty foreground for the gem-like lake sparkling in the background. The midday sun toasted the frosty morning air, coaxing the sugar maples into flower. The silence waited while a robin welcomed spring.

I knocked on the screen door. It was quiet. As I waited I spotted an old name tag stuck on a railing: "My name is Edna Staebler". I was in the right place.

I knocked again, vigorously. Maybe she wasn't home. Then I heard footsteps coming.

She looked British in her loose-knit green coat-sweater striped with coloured bands of old-fashioned Christmas candy. A pleasant ruggedness smiled across her face, and echoed in her friendly voice, in her handshake and in her hearty welcome.

The house, planned for Sunfish Lake, was fronted by wall-to-wall glass. Three steps led down into the front room and brought the lake to the house. Sunbeams and shadows danced on the multi-colored hooked rugs. The tint of late-run maple syrup mellowed the knotty pine walls and blended with the smoke-stained fireplace.

"Come out to the sun room," she said, and we stepped down into a room surrounded with glass and cluttered with furniture still dressed in winter clothing. "It hasn't been warm enough to sit out here, and the room's a mess. Can I get you a drink? I got some fresh apple cider from the market this morning — it's the last of the season."

The cloudy cider matched the maple syrup color of the knotty pine. It was chilled and good.

"Tell me," she said. "What relation are you to my former husband Keith Staebler?"

"Keith's father, Leslie, and my father's mother, Mary Staebler, were brother and sister. She died on my father's first birthday. I've had an awful time tracing her ancestors. However, I now have fourteen generations of Staeblers in my genealogy, thanks to —."

"You said you've written the first chapter of a novel. Tell me about it."

I told her about the story inspired by the old letter. "Margaret's sister Catharine married the first Louis Breithaupt — so I'm related to all the Breithaupts and most of the Staeblers. Before writing more, I wanted to visit the Kitchener-Waterloo area and get a feeling for this country, its people and its history. When I read your story, "Cooking The Evidence" *, I just had to call you."

"Did you bring the manuscript? I'd like to read it."

I gave her the story, and as she glanced through it, I continued. "I'd like to learn more about the Breithaupts. Louis and Jacob Wagner were partners when the Tannery was founded in Kitchener in 1857. I want to meet Keith, and any other Staeblers I can find. This country must be full of them."

"You should see Dottie Shoemaker, and Marnie Paisley. Marnie knows the Breithaupts well and may be related to them, and Dottie was Kitchener's librarian for years. She's nearly eighty, and has osteoporosis, but she drives downtown every day peering through the spokes of her steering wheel!"

Her sentences were punctuated with chuckles as she talked about her writings, about her experiences in Cape Breton, in Europe, in Alberta's Hutterite colony and how she kept her first manuscript in the dresser drawer for twenty-five years.

I listened, fascinated by the cadence and the smiles in her voice, recognizing the friendly one-on-one style of her cook book and her *Saturday Night* story. I marvelled once more at my good fortune and wondered who was leading me around, because I had that feeling again — the feeling I'd had when I approached the Faulkner settlement in Hastings County, when I drove through the winding roads in Andover, Massachusetts, where Edmund Faulkner had settled in 1635, and again in nearby Hespler, when I found the house where my father was born — a deep feeling that someone was leading me.

She talked about her friends — her publisher, Jack McClelland; Pierre Berton, who wrote the introduction for

* Edna Staebler, "Cooking the Evidence", Saturday Night, May 1987

Sauerkraut and Enterprise, and praised her bean salad and her use of words; my favorite Canadian author, Margaret Laurence, who had stayed at Sunfish Lake. Edna Staebler wasn't name-dropping. She was simply sharing them with me.

And I thought, *how lucky can you get?*

"I visited the Kitchener Farmers' Market this morning. Had fried sausage and sauerkraut in a bun for breakfast," I said. "My grandfather took me to the old market fifty years ago — I love it. Bought four litres of maple syrup. Hope I can get it home."

"Did you buy it from a Mennonite woman?"

"Yes. A tall, handsome, black-haired woman, with a stall under the stairway."

"That's the Sarah in my story!"

My God! Here we go again ...

"She lives about two miles from here, near Heidelberg. She and her daughters walked over for a visit last week. If you turn left at the dead end you'll see their place, just before the crossroad. There's a 'Maple Syrup for Sale' sign at the entrance to their farm."

I'd been fascinated by the Mennonites in her cookie war story and I wanted desperately to meet Bevvy and Sarah, visit their farms, capture an empathy for their way of life — the life my ancestors lived when they came to Waterloo County one hundred sixty years ago. Should I ask this fascinating woman to take me to Sarah's home, to share the friendship she enjoys with these reclusive people? Or should I just drive to their farm and buy some more maple syrup?

"Oh, look, there's a cardinal at your feeder," I said.

"Yes, he's just returned and will spend the summer here. I enjoy my birds. I used four hundred pounds of bird seed last winter. I enjoy all my visitors. During the summer months I'm never alone. You're this season's first!"

It was time to go. I'm leery of a strange car on a strange road, especially in the dark. "When will I see you again?" I asked.

"I'm going out for dinner tomorrow, and I'll be busy all day Monday. How about Tuesday?"

"Tuesday's fine. I'd like to take you out for dinner."

"Thank you, I'd enjoy that. Come early and we'll visit Bevvy and Sarah. St. Jacob's has a couple of good restaurants."

The lengthening shadows had begun to blanket Sunfish Lake, the lingering gold of the evening sun turning the cardinal's scarlet jacket to a shiny bronze as he cracked sunflower seeds for his evening meal. The yellow of the dying light flooded the cottage, tinging the knotty pine to copper ...

I took my time driving back, passing through St. Agatha, Petersburg and Heidelberg, each with a flashing stop-light at the village centre; each with a store, a filling station and an oversized church whose tall spire probed the evening sky.

Between the villages my eyes roamed the hills, followed fences. Most fields lay cornstalked in winter's garb, but the road side gloried in its newborn green, while embarrassed maples tried to hide their naked limbs with their tiny flowers.

Then I stopped near a sugar bush, to catch on film a farm silhouetted against the dying blue of the eastern sky. The huge barn dwarfed the house, the grossdoddy (the grandparent's house) and other out-buildings, guarded on both sides by sentinel-like silos. I watched the setting sun sink into a silo, then I turned and leaned against a rail fence and wondered ... *What ran through your mind, Jacob Hailer, when you watched the sunset from your woodworking shop at the corner of King and Scott Streets, so many years ago?*

I'd soon be hurtling down 401, into the turbulent bowels of Toronto, but I thought, *I'll get to know this land, and its people — my people — and Edna Staebler and her Sunfish palace. She's taking me to see Bevvy and Sarah. Everything is falling into place again. Someone must really care.*

From My Window

The Story

Margaret (Hailer) Wagner with her son Rev. L.H. Wagner
and grandson Louis (author's father)

From My Window

Hailer home, corner King and Scott Streets

AN 1849 WEDDING

Soon-to-be sixteen year old Catharine Hailer's home-made boots danced along the planked sidewalk of King Street. As she passed Erb's store, she stopped to rub the velvet nose of the horse tied to the hitching rail. "Hello, Dancer. Did you bring Uncle Herman to town? Oh! You're such a nice horse." She cuddled her freckled cheek against the horse's head and brushed at the humming flies with her chestnut-colored pigtail. The gray mare, her ears alert, nudged against her apron pocket. "No sugar today, Dancer. You old honey-horse, you take good care of Uncle Herman and see he gets home."

She bounced down Berlin, Ontario's foot-worn wooden-sidewalk towards the Hailer home, silently singing *Hippity hop to the barber shop.*

"I know I'm too old to hop," she said to herself, " and I daren't sing, but I feel so good I think I'll burst. There's Herr Schneider dozing in his favorite chair. If I'm quiet maybe I can sneak by the post office without waking him." She slowed to a tip-toe as she neared the tiny post office.

The warm July sun lazied the afternoon. As Cathie's shoes gently hissed the sidewalk, dancing maple leaves sprinkled shadows over the sleeping postmaster, bees hummed in the lilacs, a pair of crickets chirped to one another.

She was almost past the post office when Herr Schneider lifted his double chin off his chest and grinned. "You nearly by me slipped, Fraulein Hailer."

"Did I disturb your dreams, Herr Postmaster?"

"No Liebchen, I was just daydreaming, most about my dear Mary, God bless her soul. For your father a letter from Albany, New York I have. From your preacher friend Jacob Wagner I think it comes. He your sister Margaret is liking, no?"

"She's sorta sweet on him. He's a powerful speaker and Maggie has run the Sunday School the last two years."

"This morning your father, with his buggy and a spinning wheel to Waterloo I see going. Maybe before he is home coming, I closed will be. Better you the letter home take."

"He'll be back by suppertime. I'd love to take the letter home."

"Come, Liebchen, to you the letter I give."

She recognized Jacob Wagner's writing — strong broad strokes sprawled across the envelope. "Thank you, Herr Schneider. The letter is from Jacob, and Papa will be pleased you gave it to me."

As she emerged from the shade of the maple tree, she held the letter in both hands and pressed it to her bosom. Then, with a quick glance up and down dusty King Street, she put the letter to her lips to kiss it, and tucked it in her bosom. She felt a blush hide her freckles, her heart quickened, and the afternoon glowed as she floated over the planked sidewalk. She adored Jacob.

But Jacob, the saddle-back preacher, had eyes for only her sister Margaret. God's work was his first concern and, with Maggie running the Sunday School for the past two years, it was little wonder she and Jacob were together so much. *I should have spent more time in the Sunday School, but I really can't stand all those Indians. Maggie seems to love it, and Jacob hopes to save their souls. He is so handsome, with his black curly hair, those broad shoulders and the thunderous voice. No wonder he saves so many souls. The Indians call him Catogaquah, the voice that roars like the mighty Niagara. Besides, Maggie went to all of Reverend Wagner's meetings and some lasted for two and three hours. I couldn't sit still that long.*

She slowed to a walk. She'd keep Jacob to herself for a little longer. Picking her way across the dust of Scott Street, she could see Maggie on the veranda. *She's sewing again, more stuff for her hope chest. Wish she'd pay attention to Henry Umbach; he's forever hanging around Papa's shop. He'd marry Maggie tomorrow if she'd have him, then Jacob might look at me.*

Catharine reached for the letter nestled in the warmth of her bosom, and as the envelope rubbed against her breasts, her skin goosepimpled. She fumbled with the latch on the picket-fence gate. "Maggie, there's a letter from Jacob, but it's addressed to Papa, and we won't be able to open it until Papa gets back from Waterloo. You know the only reason he writes so often is that he is sweet on you."

"Don't be silly, Cathie, it's probably about the church and Reverend Wagner's next visit. Our Berlin church was the first in Upper Canada, and Papa is the presiding Elder."

"He never used to write so often. This is the third letter this year. Let's get Mama to open it."

"What are you two talking about?" asked the stern-faced Mother Hailer, as she stepped onto the veranda.

"Mama, here is a letter from Jacob. Let's open it."

"You mean Reverend Wagner. Catharine, you know I'd never open Papa's mail. I'll take care of the letter until Papa returns. You go fetch the cows, Catharine, and forget about the letter. Come, Margaret, put your sewing away and help me with supper. There's a new man in the shop today, and I think Scarface Tom and his squaw will eat here."

"Yes, Mother, but may I see the letter?" Margaret asked.

"You know we'll have to wait for your pa to open it. He won't look at it until after evening prayers. You mustn't get your hopes up about Reverend Wagner. He's totally dedicated to the work of the Lord, and besides, I don't see how he could support a wife and family. He's still a saddle-back preacher; you couldn't follow him around the circuit."

"Mother, he has a charge in Albany now and he doesn't travel nearly as much as he did."

"There are plenty of fine young men in the settlement. I noticed Henry Umbach at the prayer meeting Wednesday night. He never took his eyes off of you. He's the oldest son and he'll be taking over the farm one of these days."

"But, Mother, I want to work for the Lord, and Jacob needs help."

"Margaret, you dream too much. You could serve the Lord as a farmer's wife. Come, it's time to start supper, and I think I see your Father's buggy on the hill."

The Hailer home hummed as the afternoon shadows lengthened. Margaret shook the steaming pot of potatoes, lifted the lid and peaked at the simmering sauerkraut. Mother Hailer rolled the sausage one last time, golden-browned the first panfull, set them on the back of the stove, and filled the frying pan again. The sausage hissed their garlic aroma to meet the scent of pine sawdust from Jacob Hailer's work shop.

As Jacob climbed out of his buggy, his nose twitched at the horsey whiff of ammonia. The smell of the cow barn and the pig pen fought with the fragrance of the lilacs. The whining, foot-driven lathes tried to drown the dull, dying sound of the lazy summer day. Jacob unhitched his horse, led her to the barn door, slipped off her harness, unbridled her and with a gentle pat turned her into the pasture.

As he closed the gate, Catharine and the cows emerged from the elderberry swamp. "Papa, don't close the gate," she called. "Hurry, you lazy cows." She wasn't sure how much she dared to coax her father.

"Papa, I fetched a letter from the post office. It's from Reverend Wagner. Will you open it before supper? I love to read Reverend Wagner's letters. Do you think he is planning a trip to Berlin this summer?"

"Liebchen, never mind about letters from Reverend Wagner; just get the cows tied up and I'll help you milk. What is it that gets you girls so excited about Reverend Wagner? It must be more than the Holy Spirit, though he sure knows how to preach and garner the lost souls into the Kingdom of God. Come, let us get the milking done. I can smell that supper's almost ready."

"But the letter, Papa. When will you open the letter?"

"Not till after evening prayers, Catharine, and the letter is likely about the next church conference and really won't be of interest to you."

"Papa, I'm always interested in what Reverend Wagner does. Just because Maggie looks after the Sunday School doesn't mean the rest of us aren't interested in the Church."

"Come, Catharine, we will milk."

As the shadows stretched across the Hailer farmyard, the quiet of the dying day dulled the senses. The lathes hummed to rest; the men shed their leather aprons, washed, and headed for the kitchen.

"So, Bossy, so, Bossy," crooned Catharine, patting the brindled Swiss cow. "It's milking time again, Bossy, and you keep your tail still until I'm finished." She squatted, pulled the stool under her, and tucked her head into the warm flank of the cow. She listened to the tune the jets of milk played on the bottom of the pail; it reminded her of the joy she felt as Jacob led his meetings in song. She milked to the rhythm of a hymn, watching the froth climb the metal sides. The pail filled, and she felt the warmth creep sensously up her calves, through her knees and into her thighs, arousing her. Her small breasts filled. Her nipples pushed against her petticoat. She wondered how it would feel when she gave milk. A full sense of womanhood possessed her, and Jacob Wagner's curly black hair and his ringing voice floated through her reverie. The pail was full. The cow switched her tail. Catharine felt good all over.

She set the pail of milk on the milking table out of reach of the cats, and walked into the manger to untie Bossy. She patted her back and scratched behind her ears and around her horns.

"You're a good old cow Bossy. You like to be milked, don't you?" *I don't suppose you had any trouble growing up. You were a heifer one day, and a cow and mother the next. Do you think they'll ever let me be a woman? I'm a woman now, you know. More of a woman than Maggie and she's probably going to get married. Bossy don't you think I'd make a better wife for the Reverend than Maggie? I wish you could talk, Bossy. But I don't suppose anybody'd listen to you. Nobody listens to me. They just think I'm a young girl. I'm old enough to have a baby so why is it such a sin to think about it and feel the way I do?* "Never mind Bossy, we're all finished. You get out into the pasture and I'll see you in the morning."

As she helped her father put the milk in the cooler, she wondered why he couldn't see how changed she was. *I know other men do, even Postmaster Herr Schneider.*

In the Hailer house the workers ate before the family gathered for the evening meal. There were five girls and one boy: Margaret, Catharine, Harriet, Marion, Caroline and four-year-old Christian. Jacob sat at the head of the table with the oldest, Margaret, on his left and youngest, Christian, on his right. Using German, he asked the Lord's blessing.

They ate in silence. Nobody spoke until Father did. "So we had a letter from our friend and God's servant, Reverend Wagner."

"Yes, Papa, and Herr Schneider said the letter came from Albany in four days."

"When we came here in 1830, it took a fortnight for the mail to come from Albany, and sometimes longer. Now the Grand Trunk Railway runs from Montreal to Kingston every other day and carries the mail. The railway is supposed to be here in Berlin in a couple of years. Now that Toronto is the capital of Upper Canada, the Tories want a railway connecting it to Montreal. It's supposed to go through Berlin."

"When are you going to open the letter, Papa?"

"After prayers, Catharine."

"Can we start now, Papa?"

"Be patient, my child, and let me finish my coffee. Mother, Mrs. Schultz likes her spinning-wheel, and now she wants six ladder-backed chairs and a rocking chair to match. She asked to be remembered to you. I hear Hans Koehler is building a bigger shop in Hespler and will have twenty men working for him."

Ladder Back chair - circa 1835
made by Jacob Hailer

45

"Jacob, your spinning-wheels are the envy of all the women in the settlement, I hope you are not planning to enlarge your shop, especially with five girls in the family and only the one boy," said Mother Hailer.

"I enjoy my work, I have two good men and I still have time to serve the Lord. Amen."

"Can we have prayers now, Papa?"

"Very well, Catharine, we will begin."

They pushed the fine, hand-turned, ladder-back chairs from the table and knelt before them, elbows resting on the rush-bottomed seats, praying hands tucked under their chins. Papa prayed first, thanking God for another day and seeking His blessing for all their various endeavors. Mother Hailer prayed next, followed by Margaret's long list for the souls of almost everybody in the settlement.

Catharine sighed and quickly said, "God bless us all. Amen."

The rest of the children all copied Catharine's "God bless..." and Christian had the last Amen.

"Where's the letter, Mother?"

"I have it, Jacob. Perhaps we could read it on the veranda. It's so hot in the house. You girls get the dishes washed. Harriet, you help Margaret and Catharine in the kitchen. Marion, you get your Bible and read to the young ones. Caroline and Christian, you go with Marion to the bench on the veranda, and see you listen carefully as she reads the word of God. Come Jacob, it will be cooler on the veranda."

The sinking sun's lazy rays stole through the lower branches of the maple guarding the front yard, dappling the veranda walls with dancing shadows and lazy sunbeams. The mauve scent of lilacs drifted delicately on the quiet evening air. Somewhere a cricket chirped once, starting the rhythm of the rocking chairs. Jacob opened the letter with a craftsman's care. Mother Hailer listened as Marion read the story of Noah's Ark to the two youngest. The rattle of dishes and the giggles of the kitchen-girls echoed into the peace of the veranda air.

The rhythm of Jacob's rocker paused. He folded the single sheet of the letter, carefully placed it in its envelope and passed it to his wife. "Reverend Wagner wants to marry our Margaret. Read the letter, my dear." She unfolded the letter:

Front page of old letter in German Script - August 1849

Albany, August 22th, 1849.

Most honored Family Hailer:

I wish to greet you with the blessings of Jesus, from him that has kept me until now, and as he will keep me in marriage from eternity to eternity. Amen.

With joy I received a letter on the 16th of June that you wrote on the 12th. Thanks to the Lord I am well. Much beloved, the reason that I am writing this is as follows: I have decided to enter into Holy Matrimony since I think I will do better. Now what I want to say is this: I have decided that if circumstances are as they were when I left you, my thoughts are with our

*friendship and my wish is to have Margaret for my wife,
if she and God are willing. This is a good reason, you
know how I was when I stayed at your home, and I am
still the same. I do not think it necessary to write much
if my question to Margaret is answered. Therefore I will
write her now. You know that it will be hard for me to
meet the expense, but I will do all I can. As soon as you
receive this letter would you please write me in detail
what you want to do. I will not fail to answer you. No
matter what happens I will watch my heart until I know
your decision.*

Jacob Wagner

"Well I'm not surprised," said Mother Hailer as she returned
the letter to her husband. "Should we let Margaret read it? I see
the back side of the letter is for Margaret. Reverend Wagner
must be hard up if he couldn't afford a separate letter."

"Mother, Reverend Wagner gives us the decision, and we
must ask the Lord. Margaret has dedicated her life to Jesus, and
she should marry a man of God. She'll help spread His word
through this wilderness. But I don't like to see her go so far from
home. There were twenty-five souls in her Sunday School last
week."

"Jacob, Margaret has a mind of her own. I think we should
give her the letter. She'll never do anything against our will."

"Yes, Mother. Let us ask the Lord to help us. We'll ask for
His guidance in our bedside prayers. The Lord will lead us-- He
always has."

Catharine's head popped through the door. "Oh Maggie!
Papa's opened the letter. Come quickly. What did he say, Papa?
Is he coming soon? I hope he is."

"Catharine, will you please be quiet," said Mother Hailer.

Margaret stood in the doorway, the gentle twilight softening
her face and candling a gloss on her tightly-tamed hair. She tried
not to show her excitement as she recognized Jacob's fine Ger-

man script in the letter resting on her father's lap. She hoped Jacob was coming to Berlin soon. She missed him. She felt her face warm. *I mustn't blush. I can't let them see I care.*

Father Hailer carefully folded the letter and put it in the envelope. "Margaret, Reverend Wagner seeks our permission to marry you."

"Wunderbar!" gasped Catharine, as she tried to hide the pain that grabbed her heart. "Wh-whe-when's the wedding?"

"Catharine, will you be still?" ordered her father. "Margaret, the front page of the letter is addressed to the family, and on the back is a letter to you. Your Mother and I have read the first page, but before we give you the letter, we'll heed Reverend Wagner's request and take it to the Lord in prayer. Then, when you make your decision, you'll know how your Mother and I feel. We'll leave it until tomorrow, and with God's help you'll have our answer. Now I must go to the shop. Do Scarface and his squaws want to sleep there tonight?"

"Yes, Papa," answered Margaret. "Scarface accepted Jesus at Reverend Wagner's last visit, and they want to stay for the Sunday services. I told them they could sleep in the shop, but they'd have to be out before the men come to work."

Jacob Hailer paused at the bottom of the kitchen steps. The dying light of the western sky silhouetted the long shop and the hip-roofed barn with washed-out pink. In the deepening blue of the east, the trees in the orchard struggled to hold the cobalt tint of the fading day. In the velvet air a cowbell orchestrated the chorus of frogs bubbling from the elderberry swamp. A night-hawk, high in the sky, ceased its plaintive cry, zoomed down, then looped skyward over the barn's vane, the rush of air through its wings booming like a bass drum.

Jacob's heart warmed as his feet felt the path to the shop. Twenty years ago he had left Germany for the new land. Now his oldest would leave home. He had faith in the Lord, faith in himself, and faith in a good life for Reverend Wagner and his daughter.

The wood-smoke smell of Scarface and his women led him through the gloom to the three figures huddled by the shop door. He opened the small door and the three Indians followed him into the shop. "Chief, you are welcome to sleep in the shop tonight. Children of Jesus will always find shelter here. But Chief, why do you still have two wives?"

Herr Hailer, you're a kind man but you'll never understand how the Great Spirit lets us take the white man's God.

"Number one wife too old for papoose, but still good for work. Chief must have many children, him need young woman."

"Chief, you know the Bible says one man for one woman. Reverend Wagner married you to young Alcoma last year. You didn't tell him you had an older wife."

I told him, he didn't want to hear me. He was interested in getting more souls for his Jesus.

"Him no ask, me no tell."

"You may stay here tonight, but next time you come to Berlin you leave other wives at home. You understand?"

Herr Hailer you are kind and so is your daughter. We will be comfortable in your shop.

"Yes, Herr Hailer. Me do."

"Goodnight, Chief."

"Goodnight, Herr Hailer."

Jacob Hailer's feet retraced the foot-smoothed path to the house and stepped into the candle-lit kitchen. Margaret and Catharine stood at the bottom of the steep stairway, candle in hand, ready for bed. "Goodnight, Father," they chorused.

"Gute nacht, meine Liebschen. Come, Mother, I'm weary from my trip to Waterloo." Margaret followed her husband to their bedroom. They undressed, one on each side of the bed, their backs to each other, slipped into long flannel night gowns, and knelt in silent prayer before crawling under the foot-thick, goose-down tick.

Jacob tucked the tick under his chin and turned to Margaret. "I'm pleased that Reverend Wagner wants our Margaret. He'll make her a fine Christian husband."

"Yes, Jacob, but she'll be so far from home. I'm happy she will serve the Lord, but I'd rather she married young Umbach. If Reverend Wagner continues to ride the circuit, she'll be alone a lot. I'd like to have our first grandchildren close by. Do you think a saddle-back preacher should be married?"

"Reverend Wagner will soon be called to a church. But I don't think Margaret should wait. We have four daughters, and we can't be too fussy."

"You're right. I could see during Reverend Wagner's last visit that they were fond of each other. But saddle-back preachers aren't the best of providers; they're kind of like God's gypsies. Do you know, I think Catharine in her impulsive way is more than just fond of Reverend Wagner. Sometimes I worry about Catharine. Because we waited ten years for little Christian, you've always treated her more like a son than a daughter. If Reverend Wagner wanted to marry Catharine we wouldn't have much to say about it."

"Mother, you worry too much. The Lord will provide, my dear."

"I hope the Lord will provide enough for two, and there'll be more, you know."

"The Reverend tells me that his father is a cooper and has a thriving barrel business in Lyons, New York, and there is the family farm. There are only two boys in the family, and his brother Philip is already well established on a homestead in Wisconsin, so Reverend Wagner will likely get the farm."

"Where did you put the letter, Jacob?"

"I left it on the table. Goodnight, Mother."

"Good night, Jacob."

The two older girls slept in a small bedroom sharing the poster-bed with its corn-husk mattress on top of tightly strung ropes. Their father had turned the four ball-topped posts from the same piece of maple. Sturdy inch-thick boards joined the posts top and bottom, with three furled spindles between the boards. The round, pole-like sides, studded with knobs for the ropes, screwed into the posts, a right hand thread on one end and a left hand on the other. The corn-husk mattress rustled in protest as Catharine plunked down on her side of the bed. "I get so cross with Papa, Maggie, I could scream. He should've let you read the letter. It is your letter, isn't it?"

"Cathie, don't be upset, I'm sure Papa thinks he is doing what is God's will, and I'm sure Reverend Wagner would agree."

"Well, I don't. I saw Papa put the letter on the kitchen table. I'll wait until Pa and Ma are asleep, and I'll sneak downstairs and get it. I just can't wait till morning, and besides, I don't think it's fair."

"I couldn't read it without permission, Cathie. Please try to be patient. Pray to the Lord for help, and tomorrow will soon be here."

"You do want to marry Jacob, don't you?"

"Only if God answers our prayers and tells me to."

"Do you love Jacob? Does he tie your stomach into tight little knots and make you feel good all over?"

"My first love will always be for Our Saviour, and I'll do what He says. The Bible tells of man's lust for women. We'll wait and see what Reverend Wagner says. Good night, Catharine."

"Good night, Maggie."

Yes, Maggie, but the Bible doesn't tell us about women's feelings. I wonder if thoughts of Jacob ever arouse you like they do me? They must, but how can you be so calm? I think I'll skip prayers tonight.

I wish Jacob wanted to marry me. I wonder if it is Maggie's work in her Sunday School that appeals to him? Just being near him makes me want to touch him. I'll never forget the time I fell, trying to get into the buggy, and he caught me. I thought he gave me a little hug, and I hugged him back. I felt his warm breath on my cheek. He smelt so good and so much like a man. It almost felt like he kissed me. Do you suppose he's ever kissed Maggie? She's always so prim and proper. Goodness me! These must be thoughts of the devil, but I like them.

Maggie's sound asleep. How can she sleep with that letter downstairs? I think I'll sneak down and read it. The moon's so bright tonight I won't need a candle.

Catharine slowly pulled herself to the edge of the bed. She listened to Maggie's soft snore and the corn husks in the mattress rustling each time she moved. She stood beside the bed. Maggie hadn't stirred. The full moon slanted an elongated patch of dull silver across the bedroom floor and stretched to the small hall at the head of the steep stairs. She listened to the sleepy duet from her parents' bedroom, and creaklessly crept down the stairs.

In the creamy moonlight Jacob's letter glowed eerily on the kitchen table. She held it to her heart, and then silently opened the front door. The dew-damp veranda chilled her bare feet, the night's silence throbbed to the bubbling chorus of the swamp-frogs, and fireflies tried to brighten the scent of lilacs. On the east end of the veranda the moon drew a firm triangle, casting a shadow of the house across the lawn. Catharine stood in the moon-lit triangle and read Jacob Wagner's letter. *Doesn't sound like Jacob. But I like the ending — it means he'll be back here some-day.*

She hesitated in awe before she began the letter to "Mar-garetha", as Jacob called her sister. Her heart pounded as she read. In her mind, the letter was for her.

From My Window

Back page of German letter

Well beloved Margaretha Hailer:

Don't be affronted if I'm short in my titillations to you. I'm not doing it to treat you mean. We got to know each other at my stay with you. I have thought to get married, if it is God's will and if there is no hindrance, of which I do not know. So now decide! You know my rank and situation as much as is necessary for you to know, so you can decide what to do. This matter is an important step; firstly, it includes to be submissive to the husband, and consequently you are no more your own master, as far as it concerns the marriage. Also you have to get used to the way of life, which as you clearly know in advance, brings inconveniences and annoyances, and demands a healthy soul and body. This last point has to be confirmed by you, otherwise this important step never can be undertaken.

When my letter reaches you I expect as fast as you can your decision in a few lines. Right or wrong. If it shall be, I would—for the sake of your love—come for you, but I don't dare. First, I can't very well get away

54

*from here, and secondly, the journey costs so much. It's
impossible to travel under twenty five dollars there and
return, and that is for me alone. I wouldn't know where
to get the money. So I thought your father or your
mother could escort you as far as Rochester, then by
canal barge and in sixteen hours you would be here in
Albany. Give me an answer to this letter, I'll write
again. May your decision turn out as it will, we shall
stay friends.*

*Now, my dearest, if these lines reach you in health,
I request your kind acceptance of one who goes step in
step with God's mercy, has done nothing that would not
be right, did what his power allowed, to pass you and
your destiny into God's hands. I'll stay in any case your
well-wisher.*

Jacob Wagner

A warm halo enveloped her; she could feel Jacob Wagner
beside her as she read. Yes, she'd be prepared for the inconveniences of married life, and put up with the annoyances but she
wondered if Maggie would. Sarah Schmidt's mother had told her
daughter about those inconveniences, and Sarah had told
Catharine. *I know all about babies; they're made just the same as
the calves and baby pigs are. I'd like to have lots of children, especially if they are like my little brother, Christian. Jacob wants to be
the boss, does he? He might be big and mighty with Maggie, but not
with me!*

Somewhere an owl hooted once and ceased. She lifted her
eyes, her body tensed, and soft tears doubled the moon. A chill
shook her, and she shivered once as she pictured Maggie and
Jacob at the wedding. Slowly she folded the letter, put it into the
envelope and pressed it to her lips. *I love you, Jacob, and I always will. I'm sure Maggie will say yes. Papa has to get us girls
married as soon as he can. I just hope he makes Jacob come to
Berlin to marry Maggie. Be terrible not to have a wedding! If Mag-*

gie has to go to Rochester to meet Jacob, maybe I could go with her, and get a chance to see him once more.

She wrapped her arms around herself, pulled them up against her breasts, turned her back on the moon and tiptoed to the door. The veranda floor chilled her feet. She paused at the door. Moonlight had turned the corner of the house and found the first lilac tree. Fireflies flickered in the mauve-scented shadows, and the frogs still sang. Standing in the doorway, she breathed once, deeply, filling her heart and body with the silver scent of lilacs. "For you, Jacob, and for our love," she whispered, "Lilacs will forever soothe my soul."

The open door framed the picture. The soft patina of silver mixed the lilac mauve to a delicate softness, and the fireflies sparkled the canvas with tiny stars. The image and her love nestled into the depths of her aching heart. Forever after, the scent or colour of a lilac would blush her cheek and stir the woman in her soul.

Firmly, yet slowly, she closed the door, closed out the silvered radiance of the night, and closed Jacob Wagner from her life.

The Hailer household awakened with the dawn. Jacob kindled a fire in the kitchen stove and soon had the kettle singing. Mother Hailer entered the kitchen and warmed her morning-cold hands over the stove. "I found my answer to Reverend Wagner's request," she said. "The Lord told me to give them my blessings. I don't think He could have found a better partner for our God-fearing daughter."

"I never had any doubts about the Reverend. I don't know what he will have to say to our Margaret, but he couldn't have found a better woman for a preacher's wife. She'll be down soon. Give her the letter and she may tell us something before we have morning prayers."

The whole family was at the breakfast table. Father Hailer asked the blessing and they ate in silence. Jacob Hailer didn't like to linger over their morning meal and often called for prayers before the sleepy children had finished. "Before we have prayers

I think Margaret might like to tell us what Reverend Wagner had to say. You've had time to read the letter. Have you anything to tell us?"

"Papa, don't make Maggie..." Catharine stuttered.

"Catharine, will you please be quiet and let Margaret tell us," said her Father.

"Thank you, Father. I've read both of the Reverend's letters. I know I have your blessing, and Mother's, and I've sought God's will in my prayers. I feel humble and grateful that one of God's servants should want me for his wife, and..."

"You're going to marry him in Rochest... Won't we have a wedding?"

"Catharine, will you be still and let your sister finish?"

"Father, I feel it's God's will that I join Reverend Wagner as his wife and his companion in the church. In his letter he says he can't afford to come to Berlin for the wedding, and wants me to go to Rochester."

"Maggie, don't you do everything Reverend Wagner wants. You should be married here. We'd all miss out on the wedding— the family's first wedding."

"Catharine, I won't speak to you again. Another interruption and you'll have to leave the table. What's your decision, Margaret?"

"Papa, I'm going to marry Reverend Jacob Wagner. I'll meet him in Rochester if need be, but I think he should come at least to Fort Erie. We could stay with Uncle Henry Riehl and Aunt Anna."

"We must write Reverend Wagner today and accept his proposal. Margaret, you write the letter and tell him you're willing to meet him in Fort Erie, and ask him to suggest a date. Mother, you write to your brother and tell him of our plans. Catharine, there will be no wedding in Berlin unless the Reverend changes his mind, so stop frowning. Now let us pray. Already the men in the shop are working."

The wedding plans were resolved when Louis Breithhaupt dropped by the Hailer home. Louis, and his father Liborius, had a tannery in Buffalo, and they made periodic buying trips to Canada. Louis was a good friend of Jacob Wagner and had met the Hailer family. He knew Jacob intended to ask Margaret to marry him, and he stopped by Hailer's shop the day after Margaret had made her decision.

With Louis Breithaupt's help and letters to Albany, Buffalo and Fort Erie, it was decided Jacob Wagner would come to Buffalo and stay with the Breithaupts. Jacob Hailer, Margaret and Catharine (much to her delight) would go to Fort Erie and stay with the Riehls, Jacob Hailer's brother-in-law. The couple would be married in Buffalo at the home of Liborius Breithaupt, God and the elements willing, on Friday the 14th of September, 1849.

The mist of an early autumn morning hugged the edge of the orchard and threatened to cover the pasture. The Hailer family gathered around the heavily loaded democrat like phantoms in the shadowless glimmer of dawn. There were hugs and sighs, and tears and cries, until finally Jacob said, "Come, Margaret, finish your goodbyes and get into the front seat. Catharine, you sit in the back. It's almost daylight, and if we are to reach Buffalo in time for the wedding we'd better get started."

The team pulled out of the yard onto King Street and down the hill as the new day blew out the stars. Somewhere a dog barked twice and a rooster crowed. Catharine's skin tingled with excitement as she cuddled in her cubby-hole of blankets.

A silly ditty kept running through her head in time to the rhythm of the horses' jingling harness.

Hippity hop to the barber shop

I'm off to Maggie's wedding

I'm not to be the bride you see,

But I'll be at the wedding.

The bumps of the corduroy road jarred the song from her mind, reminding her of the ache in her heart. Part of her heart — not broken, but cracked and scarred — would forever belong to

Jacob. *Oh! If they'd only let me be a woman. Would I still be plunged from the height of happiness to the dungeons of despair? Maggie says it's a struggle to stop the devil from taking over your soul, but if you have faith and love Jesus, the Holy Spirit will fill your heart with happiness. Sometimes I think Maggie's love for Jacob is overshadowed by her love of God. Maggie seems so sure of herself. I suppose she's been sure of Jacob ever since she was saved.*

She watched the wheel of the buggy and wondered how far it went each time it turned. *Is it taking me closer to Jacob, or does each turn seal the pledge I made the night I read Maggie's letter?* The jingle of the horses' traces broke her reverie, and the hippity-hop ditty returned, soothing her troubled mind. *Fiddlesticks! I won't think about it any more. It's a lovely day and it will soon be my turn to sit up front with Papa.*

After driving for three or four hours, they rested and fed the horses and themselves. The sun hung low as the inland sea of Lake Ontario broke the horizon. They could see the high-rigged ships in Hamilton's harbour.

They spent the night in a hostelry on Hamilton's waterfront. On their second day the road followed the shoreline of the lake, and a strong wind off the water chilled the passengers but gave the horses a flyless day, and by late evening they found the farm of Herman Gottmann near the settlement of St. Catharine. Herman and Jacob had crossed the ocean together with some of the Riehl family.

The third day they left the shores of Lake Ontario and cut cross-country to Niagara Falls, where they fed and rested the horses.

"We should be in Fort Erie by early afternoon," said Jacob as the thunder of the falls fell behind the democrat. Catharine was sitting up front with her father.

"Isn't it exciting, Maggie? By this time tomorrow you'll be a married woman. Aren't you kinda scared?"

59

"Not really, Cathie. I asked the Lord to help me and he calms me and gives me strength to be patient."

"But the thought of even seeing Reverend Wagner excites me and I'm not getting married. Your heart must skip a beat or two and pound a little faster."

"Catharine, let your sister be. She has enough on her mind without your chatter."

"I'm sorry Maggie, but I'm so excited. Papa, tell me about Uncle Henry and Auntie Anna. Uncle Henry is Mama's brother, isn't he?"

"Yes, Catharine, he is. Now I'd like to have some peace and quiet for a while. We'll be by ourselves on the trip home and I'll tell you all about the Riehl family and the Hailers too."

"I'm sorry, Papa. I didn't mean to be a nuisance."

"Sehr gut, Leibschen."

The Riehl household bubbled with the joy and excitement of the wedding. They dined and laughed; they prayed and sang spicy songs, and some of the girls cried.

Reverend Wagner took a canal barge at Albany and traveled up the Erie Canal to Buffalo, where he spent the night before the wedding at the home of Liborius Breithaupt. He had known the Breithaupts since the family came from Germany in 1844, and he was happy to see his good friend Louis.

On the morning of the fourteenth of September, Jacob Hailer and his daughters caught the first ferry from Fort Erie to Buffalo. Reverend Wagner and Louis Breithhaupt met them at the dock. They led the girls and their father to a fine, double-seated buggy with a shining team of grays.

As they drove down Buffalo's busy waterfront, with the two young men up front, Catharine's eyes were glued to the stocky back of Jacob Wagner. Her heart ached as she remembered the night she'd read his letter and dreamed it was for her.

Suddenly she awakened. The spirited horses had shied at a paper blown across the road. They'd bolted, and headed for the ditch. The jolt threw Catharine back against her father's shoulder. She almost screamed as she watched Louis rein in the team and bring them back to the road.

It was the first time she'd really noticed the twenty- two year-old Louis Breithaupt. *He did a wonderful job of controlling those horses and he is almost as handsome as Jacob. He's not as broad-shouldered as Jacob, and his black hair isn't curly, but he's taller and kind of princely looking. But they all think I'm so young! Louis's twenty-two, I think, and I know Jacob's twenty-four. I suppose they think I'm too young to be a woman. I'm more womanish than Maggie. I see lots of boys looking at my bosom, and men too. Oh! The wedding's so exciting! I'm so happy Papa let me come. Maybe he thinks I might find a beau. Well, there's Louis Breithaupt* . . .

Margaret Hailer and Jacob Wagner were married in the home of Liborius Breithaupt. Catharine stood with her sister Margaret and Louis Breithaupt was Jacob's best man. They were married in the forenoon, and after a dinner of German and Mennonite foods, the newlyweds boarded a canal barge for the three-and-half day trip to Albany.

Catharine and Louis Breithaupt drove the newlyweds to the locks to get the canal boat, Catharine sitting up front with the handsome Louis. All through the wedding and the dinner her heart ached, and she almost broke into tears every time she looked at Jacob Wagner. All hope was gone. Her love for the handsome preacher and her dreams lay like flailed grain on a deserted granary floor. If she could only separate the grain from the chaff.

Jacob Hailer and Catharine stayed with the Breithaupts for the rest of the day and the night. She was impressed by their home and the fine European furnishings the family had brought from Germany.

Liborius and his family had been in the tanning business for several generations. Liborius had been sent to America to investigate the business opportunities. He spent a year before he picked Buffalo for the family venture. The busy Erie Canal and the Great Lakes connected New York to Chicago. It made Buffalo a gateway to the rich hide markets of the prairie buffalo. In 1844 he'd moved his family from their Allendorf home in Germany to a fine new home in Buffalo.

Catharine loved the gracious home and the warm hospitality of the Breithhaupt family. Louis had taken her and her father for a tour of Buffalo's growing townsite, showed her the tannery, and stopped at a small river front cafe for coffee. She felt important sitting beside Louis as he drove the spirited grays through Buffalo's bustling streets.

The next morning Louis took Catharine and her father to the ferry. At the ramp Louis shook hands with her father. "Goodbye, Herr Hailer, I will see you the next time I'm in Berlin."

"Auf weidersehen, Louis, und danke Sie!"

He turned to Catherine and took both her hands. "Goodbye Cathie, I'm so happy you could come to the wedding. I enjoyed being with you, and wish you could stay longer."

She felt him squeeze her hands and she squeezed his. She lifted her eyes to his princely face and caught his eyes as they moved from her bosom to her face. Her whole body trembled; her heartbeat quickened, and she could feel a blush override her freckles. "Goodbye Jac... Louis." she sighed, turned and ran onto the ferry.

She didn't look back. She shuddered, tripped and almost fell as a wave of passion flooded through her being, flinging her frustrations of childhood high upon the beach of experience. She'd never be a little girl again. Louis knew she was a woman.

L - R: Alma (Bean) Bender, Sarah (Moyer) Wagner, Rev.
L. H. Wagner, Florence Bean, Florence Wagner, Wesley
Bean, Margaret (Hailer) Wagner

From My Window

Family

Gordon and Ivy Wagner's Family - Christmas 1949
Keith, Shirley, Smokey (Lorne) and Linda

From My Window

LEAVING HOME

Shirley, our third child and second daughter, left home three times. Each time I watched her go she took a little of my heart with her.

Everybody loved Shirley: her teachers, the milkman, the butcher, the baker, her sister, her brothers, her mother and I. Some people love you and tell you. Some people show their love for you. The special few are living love itself. Shirley loved everyone unconditionally. As a small child sitting on my lap, she would snuggle close to me, let me rub my cheek against her soft, curly blonde hair. This small, sweet girl so warmed my heart that I wanted to keep her close to me forever.

She was four the first time she left. We had shared a good farm-grown dinner with friends and their two young boys.

As they said good night at the front door, Shirley said, "I want to go with Bobby so I can ride his bike."

After our friends left I suggested, "If you're so crazy about Bobby's bike, perhaps you'd like to go and live with them."

Minutes later she appeared at the front door warmly tucked into her parka, a bag of night clothes under her arm, and calmly announced she was going to Bobby's house.

"Don't let her go, Dad!" screamed her brother Keith. "Stop her, Dad! Stop her!"

"Hey, it's dark out there," I warned her, "and it's two miles to Bobby's house!" I watched in amazement as she went out the door and started down the driveway. I called her but she continued towards the road. I had to catch her and carry her back. That time my damaged heart quickly healed.

That same year we had moved to the Flying W, a five-acre farm on the outskirts of Courtenay. Keith was six, Linda five, and Smokey (Lorne) three. Our farm and the neighbour's twenty-five acres gave them an open pasture, a clump of big fir trees and a dense swamp for play. They gloried in their tree houses, secret trails, hide-outs and a pond. In the winter the pond became big enough to float a raft and just deep enough to top any size of rubber boots. Wet feet became so common I finally stopped mending rubber boots. Better to let the water drain out of the holes so the children were no longer sloshing around in water-filled boots.

The farm had a barn with a hay loft, a wood shed, a sawdust shed, a garage, chickens and chicks, ducks and ducklings, a cow with a calf, pigs, turkeys, and even bees. Then one day we found a horse.

The ad said, "Pack horses for sale, $25 and up." We all piled into the cranky 1927 Chrysler and found the farm. Five or six horses grazed in the winter pasture. They had spent the summer packing gear for people visiting the Forbidden Plateau. Shirley spotted Trixie. She was black with a white star on her forehead and stood fourteen hands.

"She's good with children," the owner said, "Used to be a circus horse and still knows some of the tricks." He showed us how she could count, and how she would lie down and roll over.

"What do you want for her?" I asked.

"Twenty five."

"Give you twenty."

"No."

"Twenty-two fifty?"

"OK," he replied.

"How will we ever find the money to pay for her?" I asked the wide-eyed kids.

"We'll pay for her with our allowance!" chorused three of them. Smokey didn't vote.

"It's a deal," I said and shook hands.

Trixie came home on a Sunday. I had warned the children they'd have to find some way to buy and pay for any tack they wanted. I couldn't afford the price of a saddle. When I came home from work on Monday I was surrounded at the gate.

"Dad, Mr. Lanyon has an old saddle he says we can have for twenty-five dollars. Can we get it, Dad?"

"Sure. If you can find a way to pay for it. Remember our agreement."

Next day I was late and the family had started supper without me. "How did the deal with the saddle go?" I asked as I joined them.

"Mr. Lanyon had to get some new buckles and a strap and now he wants fifty dollars for it," a crestfallen Keith reported.

"But he'll take two dollars down and two dollars a month," an excited Shirley explained. "All the kids want to ride Trixie. We could charge two cents a ride, or get a pop bottle or a beer bottle."

"Okay! I'll give you the down payment. It will take a year to pay for it."

Shirley's love soon won Trixie's. She rode her, curried her and even slept with her. One summer day I spotted Shirley with an old blanket and pillow, headed for the pasture. "What's the blanket for?" I asked.

"Trixie and I are gonna ride the range today and I reckon we might not make it back by nightfall."

"What's the pillow for? Cowboys don't use pillows."

"Oh! that's my saddle." I watched her as she approached the grazing horse. She fed Trixie a treat, and had her lie down. Shirley spread the blanket against Trixie's shoulder, tipped her straw hat over her eyes and drifted over her dreamland range.

"Look, Dad, isn't he cute? Mom says to ask you if I can keep him?" In her arms she cuddled the homeliest part Kerry-blue pup I'd ever seen. He was so homely he was cute. We'd just lost our black Lab, Kelly, and Pedro filled an aching void.

But Pedro was a girl. And six months later Shirley midwifed, mothered, and trained six of Pedro's pups and found homes for all of them.

As a teen-ager her love grew, gathering new friends — girlfriends and boyfriends. We left the farm. Our rumpus room jumped and jived, and Shirley served cinnamon toast and tea.

When Sandy, a native girl, failed to cope with racial discrimination, Shirley stood with her. She baby-sat for a doctor's children and became one of the family. During a brief hospital stay she shared a room with an elderly lady, and when Mrs. Bond died she remembered Shirley in her will.

Her beauty flowered. Her eyes sparkled, her voice sang and she moved with grace. Unaffected love twinkled in her eyes, sang in her words and danced all around her.

She left home for the second time when she exchanged her student-nursing career for marriage. Her love for Ray couldn't wait. I was watching a football game when Shirley and Ray burst through the door. Ray was supposed to be in Vancouver at U.B.C., Shirley at the Royal Jubilee Hospital in Victoria.

"What are you doing here?" I asked in my surprise.

"Shirley's three months pregnant!" Ray stammered.

It shook my Puritan ethics. This can't be — not lovable Shirley! My self-righteousness exploded, "Well, you're not getting married."

When the shock subsided and calmer minds prevailed, Ray and Shirley were married. Shirley quit her half-completed nursing course and Ray continued at university.

Shirley's love flourished with the ecstasy of marriage. Love bubbled from her soul. It overflowed to us, to her friends, and to her animals. Shirley always had time for people. In time she gave us three loving grandchildren: Jacqueline, named after Ray's father, killed in the war, Nicole and then Jordan.

I remember the trip Shirley and I took to Alberta for her grandparent's diamond wedding anniversary. Her mother and her sister drove; because of business I had to fly.

"Want to come?" I asked Shirley. She'd love to. Strangers stared as they watched a middle-aged man and his young companion holding hands as we walked through the Calgary Stampede. We loved each other, and it showed all over. My heart still swells as I recall that trip. Beautiful!

The third time Shirley left home was the last. We were aware that she and Ray were having serious marital problems. In August, 1973, she brought Jacqui, nine, Nicole, eight, and Jordie, four, to visit us in Comox.

She wasn't her usual vibrant self. We assumed she was worrying about the breakdown of her marriage. As late August approached, her depression grew. She arranged to have Jacqui and Niki attend school in Comox and she rented a small cottage on the beach. She loved the water and the children enjoyed the ocean and their nearby cousins, Raphael and Kelsey.

Finally she went to the family doctor — her baby-sitting friend. He thought she had a new virus and gave her an antibiotic. But her condition continued to worsen, and she was forced to move in with Cheryl and Smokey. She was too sick to care for herself and her family.

A few days later Cheryl called me at work. "Gordon, you'll have to take Shirley to the hospital. She's really miserable."

"I'll be right out."

Shirley responded to the tender loving care of St. Joseph's. Her love shone through the aches and pains. Her sister Linda was getting married in two weeks. "I'll be out of here by then, Dad," she promised. "Let's see — what'll I wear?"

Just before the wedding I stopped to see Shirley and found her in double isolation. I had to dress in a hospital gown and wear a mask before I could enter the room. "They're not going to let me out for the wedding, and I don't like being in a room by myself. But I can see the roof of your house, and that helps. How are the kids, Dad? I really miss them. It's been two weeks you know."

"After supper I'll bring them to the lawn below your window. You'll be able to see them and probably hear them."

"Oh, thanks Dad. That will be wonderful. Here's a kiss and a big hug for you," she said as she threw me a kiss and gave me a pretended hug.

When we returned from Linda's wedding it was obvious Shirley was not responding to her treatments. I stopped Dr. Power in the hospital hall. "Phil, have you found out what's the matter with Shirley?"

"We don't know. We're running some more tests. We're having difficulties because of the staph infection."

"Is it serious, Phil? Could it be leukemia?"

"I'm hoping it isn't. Her infection is so advanced we can't find an antibiotic to fight it, and we're having trouble with her blood cultures. It doesn't look good, Gordon."

I knew he'd have exhausted every avenue before admitting defeat. Since Shirley's baby-sitting days, her love in the Power family was well-rooted.

I can still feel the anguish that tore my heart. This couldn't be happening to our Shirley. Not to the beautiful twenty-seven year old mother of our three grandchildren! But it was. The raging fever racked her. We tried to ease her pain with soothing baths and cold compresses as she slowly slid away. "It isn't fair. It isn't fair," she moaned.

As she fought to live, I tried to cuddle her weakening body and tell her how much I loved her.

Each day we'd bring her children to the lawn. Each day we'd try not to cry as we reminisced about Trixie, Pedro and the farm, about playing cowboys and Indians. We relived those happy hours, laughed about the time she tried to leave home to live with Bobby.

She longed to visit Kye Bay again, so Keith recorded the beach-sounds of crashing waves, screaming seagulls and laughing children and brought Kye Bay to her bedside. Shirley revelled in the seaside symphony.

October came. Summer was gone, the days grew shorter, the maple tree near the hospital shed its last leaves. Shirley slowly faded; her time was running out. She knew and we knew. Her strength was nearly gone. In the early morning hospital silence on Friday, the nineteenth , we gathered around her bed, pouring our heart's love to help her on her new journey. Her hand gently pressed mine, as though from a distance — like a little girl turning to wave good bye, as she started down the road to school.

Sister Elaine came in and suggested that we wait in the sun-room. We were standing there in the darkened room watching the new day awake the eastern sky when she came back and quietly told us Shirley was gone.

We walked home. As the reverence of a new day flowed across Comox Bay, we could feel Shirley's love searching for new souls with whom to share its brightness.

Now the beauty of her being, the love and joy she gave to all who knew her, are treasured memories that ease an aching heart.

LETTER TO MY SON

Courtenay, B.C.
Sunday, 5 March 1978

Good Morning Keith:

For the past several weeks I've been trying to find the right time, the right words and the courage to tell you the thoughts that have being troubling my mind. I woke early this morning and decided this is the time.

It's a fine morning. I breakfasted with the sunrise. I sat at our kitchen window watching the sun birth a new day. The delicate first light gently lifted the night blanket off Comox Bay and the Beaufort Mountains, uncovered the Glacier and revealed a new coat of snow fringing the mountain tops. Dozing ducks yawned and flapped to life. Seagulls glided through the eerie grayness to greet the new day. Colours borrowed from

74

red roses, cranberry glass and baby pinks chased each other across the bay and tinted the frosty fringe of the mountains. A gentle breeze scattered rubies across the dancing waters. The brightening dawn's magic hued the fading rubies to flashing diamonds. As the gray sky azured to cloudless blue the diamonds turned to sparkling sapphires.

On a day like today in March thirty-four years ago I was in the Airforce stationed at Terrace, when I got an unexpected flight to Comox. You, Linda, and your Mother were living with your Aunt Mae, near the Tsolum school. I found you in bed with pneumonia, a small, sick, skinny little boy. My heart ached as I held you in my arms, kissed your fevered face and whispered my love to you. You're almost thirty-six now, a strong, handsome and intelligent man and your body is again being ravaged with pain. I haven't hugged you or told you I love you for years. I want to tell you now.

I remember our years on the farm. Good years, when we all worked hard to provide for our growing family. Remember when we bought Trixie and you dealt with Mr. Lanyon for a saddle? Your first business transaction. He wanted twenty-four dollars and you got it for two dollars down and two dollars a month. Remember your determination to become a long distance runner? My, how you trained and then came up lame on the day of the race. You ran the race despite the pain and you placed second. Remember the year you did the surveys for Elk River Timber and got three deer? The last buck was high with the scent of rut. You had hamburger (or buckburger) made. You'd fry it for an after-school snack. It smelled horrible and I finally had to insist you cook your venison-burgers on the outdoor barbecue. I remember the Christmas your Mother gave me the stereo and you built the cabinet for it. You did a great job.

I'm proud of your talent but never told you. I boasted about you to my friends but failed to tell you. I'm prone to criticize or say nothing, as if the lack of criticism can somehow be understood as praise.

We men are so reluctant to show affection, as if a handshake could replace a hug, or a tear shed disgrace our fabled manhood. Are fathers and sons not supposed to love each other?

I'm thankful and proud you stayed in the Comox Valley and made our family land surveying business your business. Thankful you chose lovely Sylvia to be your wife and the mother of Leona and Kathy. Proud of the skillful and industrious man and the fine surveyor you have become.

But why haven't I told you how good you are? I'm ashamed of my thoughtlessness. It's no solace that I'm no worse than ninety-nine percent of fathers.

I'm particularly proud of you as a land surveyor who strives for perfection. Your surveys and your name will endure forever in the records of the Land Title Office of British Columbia.

I know as you lie there, day after day, fighting a battle that has lasted seven years, a fight so heavily weighted against you, that you must be concerned for the future of your family. Fear not. Our love will care for your loved ones. Fear not for their material needs. Fear not for the love and tenderness they need now and will need in the future. Remember we love you and hope to see you well again.

I try to be brave when I visit you. It isn't fair that our son — the strong man, the devoted father and the talented surveyor -- should suffer those dreaded headaches day after day. I marvel at your strength as I strive to ease your pain and hope my love will help.

*It's taken time and tears to tell you of my love. I
care so much. I hope this letter will help in the trying
days ahead. I'll forever be proud of Gordon Keith Wagner, British Columbia Land Surveyor. My son.*
Your Dad.

Epilogue:
Keith Wagner died of cancer on the 27th of April, 1978, two
days before his thirty-sixth birthday.

A BRAND NEW LEG

Gordon? Harry Woolrich here. We've run into a problem
with Ivy's leg. The femoral artery's damaged. Dr. Sexton's
on his way from Nanaimo. He'll operate as soon as he gets here.
We need your consent. Could you get here right away?"

Harry had been our family doctor for almost twenty years.
Ivy had had a varicose vein in one leg stripped several years
before. Now he was doing the other leg. Probably he nicked the
artery just behind the knee. I was at St. Joseph's Hospital in
minutes.

Ivy, groggy and reeking of ether, lay with her right leg pil-
lowed high and packed with ice. I couldn't find the doctor, but I
found the head nurse. "What have you done to my wife's leg?" I
asked.

"All I know is they've had some trouble. Mrs. Wagner will be
going to the operating room as soon as Dr. Sexton arrives. We
need your permission for this second operation."

"What the hell have they done to her?"

"I don't know. You'll have to see Dr. Woolrich."

She paged Dr. Woolrich but there was no response. I signed that damned permission and I'll never know why. I guess I had that implicit trust we all seem to have in the glorified profession of medicine.

I checked the hospital at one o'clock. Ivy was in the operating room.

I phoned at two and again at three. "Mrs. Wagner is still in the O.R. We'll call you as soon as they're finished."

Somehow the afternoon passed. At five the hospital called. "Mr. Wagner? This is Dr. Sexton. I've just finished. Could you come to the hospital?"

Leading me into a small cell-like room, he motioned me to a chair. He sat down on the other side of a chipped enamel table, pushed back the heavy lock of black, untamed hair from his eyes. He looked exhausted.

"Damn tough afternoon," he said. "The femoral artery was damaged in the groin area. I spliced it with a vein from the left thigh. It should hold. I want to take Mrs. Wagner back to Nanaimo where I can keep an eye on her. I've made arrangements for an ambulance —"

"What happened? How was the artery damaged?"

"I don't know. You'll have to get that information from Dr.Woolrich, or from the hospital."

He's being evasive. Doctors and Masons never tell. "You mean you're not going to tell me."

He pushed the unruly hair, " No er-er-er — Mrs. Wagner is in no danger, but she could lose some toes."

Lose her toes!

"The blood supply to her right leg was cut off for several hours. It's like a frost bite. Her thigh is starting to regain its warmth, and if things go as they should ..."

I was stunned. *Splice an artery? Lose her toes? Stripping a vein is routine. What in the hell did they do?*

With all the family gone except Smokey, our youngest, Ivy had gone back to teaching. She was enjoying her kindergarden classes; that's why she was having her leg fixed during the holidays.

When I got home the phone was ringing. It was Dr. Woolrich. "Gordon, we've decided to take Ivy to Victoria, to Dr. Ralph Smith, a cardiovascular surgeon. The ambulance is ready to leave."

"Why? What's the bloody trouble *now?*"

"We think it's best. Smith's a specialist in vascular medicine. I'll talk to you later."

I arranged for someone to look after my survey business and by nine was on my way to Victoria. At least there, I'd have someone to turn to — our daughter Linda was a nurse at the Royal Jubilee Hospital .

It's three hours or better to Victoria and I pulled into the Emergency of the Royal Jubilee a little after midnight.

"Do you have a Mrs. Wagner here?" I inquired.

"Mrs. Wagner? Are we suppose ..."

"Yes — where the hell is Mrs. Wagner?" snapped a short, dapper young man. "We've been waiting for her since nine."

"She left Comox at six. I didn't leave until nine and I never passed an ambulance. Maybe they took her to Nanaimo. I'll phone — "

"I'm Dr. Ralph Smith . *I'll* phone!"

I listened. He was abrupt, demanding and just barely polite. "They had to take her into Nanaimo for a blood transfusion. She should be here any minute."

Dr. Smith met the ambulance at the entrance, barking orders. Her bad leg had slipped off the side of the narrow stretcher. "Watch what you're doing to that woman's leg," he yelled. He helped move her onto the hospital stretcher and wheel her into emergency.

Minutes later, with two interns in tow, he followed the stretcher down the hall. He stopped as he passed. "Mr. Wagner, there's nothing you can do here. Leave your phone number at the desk and I'll call you the minute I finish." He, his voice and Ivy vanished behind the swinging doors.

You're in good hands now, Ivy. Thank God!

I checked into a hotel but I couldn't sleep. *Lose her toes? She looked like she'd almost lost her life, when they took her out of that two by four ambulance. What in the hell has happened?*

At five in the morning I couldn't wait any longer. I phoned the hospital and the night-soft voice of a nurse said, "Just hold on, Mr. Wagner, I'll check."

What a kind voice she has, for five in the morning ...

"They're still in the O.R. But we have your number, Mr. Wagner, and I know Dr. Smith will call you."

At seven the phone rang. "We've just finished, and Mrs. Wagner is as good as can be expected. She's in no danger. I'd like to see you in my office at three this afternoon."

Linda was on duty when I got to the hospital at nine. News travels through a hospital like a prairie fire and she said, "I heard about this mess when I came to work, but I didn't know it was Mom. What happened?"

I filled her in, and she said, "She'll be heavily sedated, but I've switched wards, and I'll keep a close watch on her." She took me to her mother's room, and held my hand while I kissed Ivy's fevered face. I could feel the strength of family flowing through our souls. I needed her ...

The sign read *Dr. Ralph C. Smith M.D. F.R.C.S. Cardiovascular Surgeon* .

"I don't know how this happened," he said, "and I won't - - until I get a report from Comox. But somebody bungled. The splice Dr. Sexton did is fine, and the thigh is getting a fair supply of blood. But the artery that takes blood to the calf was damaged. We repaired it, but ..."

He paused, then asked, "Do you know anything about the sympathetic nervous system?"

80

"I know it controls the involuntary reactions of the body, and lies deep inside, along the backbone."

"That's right. It controls the contraction and expansion of the blood vessels. We have to get all the blood we can to the damaged areas, so we went in and cut the nerve controlling the expansion in the right leg."

He paused again, and in a quiet voice said, "I just wish I'd had her twelve hours earlier."

"Dr. Smith , I understand all that, but what the ..."

"I really don't know. I've done everything I can do. I'd send her any place in Canada or the U.S. if I thought it would help." He rose, brisk again. "I start my rounds at seven tomorrow morning. I'll be at Mrs. Wagner's room at nine. I'll see you there."

I soon learned Dr. Smith was one of Canada's top cardiovascular surgeons. He demanded, and got, the best for his patients. Nurses jumped when he spoke. He wasn't liked, but he was respected.

He met me at Ivy's bedside. "Nurse, I told you those bedclothes are not to touch Mrs. Wagner's leg. Get a frame over it. And don't give me any excuses — just do it. *Now!*"

"Yes, Dr. Smith !"

I followed him to the sun-room. "Sit down," he said, and took a seat near me.

"It doesn't look good. I'm going to have to amputate. Probably above the knee." Unconsciously he drew his hand across his knee in a knife-like gesture.

I still cringe when I think of it. I gasped, "Oh! my God ..."

"Mrs. Wagner's thigh is warming, but there's no circulation below the knee. We won't be in a hurry. There's nothing to lose by waiting."

What could I do? I sat, watching her return to the real world, watching as the room filled with flowers, talking to people who came to see our Ivy — the girl with the "toothpaste" smile.

I wondered what she knew. You don't tell a woman she's going to lose her leg. I felt the warmth of life creep over her knee. The chill left her ankle and I began to hope. But her foot looked black.

I raged and I cried. I tried to help. I held her hand, soothed her brow. But how the hell do you save a leg? You curse and swear but it doesn't help. All you can do is love and wait.

On the fourth day Dr. Smith took me to the sun-room again. "We're going to amputate tomorrow and we'll have to tell Mrs.Wagner. I've booked the O.R. for tomorrow morning, and we'll tell her tonight, so she won't have all day to think about it. I'll be here at nine this evening, and I want Linda here."

Linda and I met Dr. Smith in the hall. "I don't want to be there when you tell Mom."

"Linda, you'll soon be a registered nurse; you have to be able to do this." So we choked back our tears and stood together while Dr. Smith told Ivy she'd lose her leg.

Ivy took it better than any of us. " I figured you'd be doing something like that, but at least I'm still here and I'm feeling better every day. It won't be any worse than having a baby," and she flashed her bright, brave smile.

They did the amputation well below the knee. It took weeks to heal the stump, to learn to use a wheel chair, to graduate to crutches, and one-leg-it to the bathroom with a well-balanced hop. I saw more smiles than tears as she fought her way to health.

Dr. Woolrich came to see her. He tried to tell her, in his shy and quiet way, how terrible he felt. And Ivy, with more love and courage than anyone should have, said, "Don't feel bad, Dr. Woolrich. Just remember all the good you've done for people all these years."

The day came when she was to be fitted for a prosthesis. That's a brand new leg, you know. She'd been tied to wheel chairs, crutches and the bunny hop for too damn long. She'd dreamed of walking as she used to walk, of dancing again and wearing attractive clothes.

We went to Pentland's Prothesis Clinic in Vancouver. They made a mould to fit her stump. "Come back tomorrow and we'll try it on," said Albert. "We'll have you walking before you know it."

We arrived at Pentlands excited and full of hope — today she'd walk again, be nearly whole again. Ivy and Albert disappeared, and I sat trying to read a year-old *Time* while they fitted her brand-new leg. Then they called me in to see.

Some things sizzle your mind like a branding iron. You wear the scar forever.

Poor Ivy stood between the walking rails, her eyes full of tears. Attached to her leg was the goddamnest contraption I'd ever seen.

A shiny steel pipe extended from her stump to a shoe-covered foot. A set of ugly adjusting screws clung to the pipe, one at the stump and the other at the ankle, like valves on a steam pipe. My God! What a horrible substitute for a woman's sexy leg.

Anger ripped across my heart. *What the hell have you done to this beautiful human being? You bastards, with all your medical know-how. Is this the best you can do?*

"Take that damn thing off and let's get the hell out of here," I said.

But Ivy gritted her teeth and walked the length of the rails to a seat, where they unstrapped the monster from her footless leg.

Two weeks later we hobbled back for another fitting. Neither of us wanted to go. This time when they called me in Ivy wore her sparkling smile and both her legs were clad in smooth stockings and neat new shoes. I could hardly tell the tell the good leg from the prothesis.

Ivy spent four months in hospital wards. Now another battle started. Or perhaps it started when I found out what had happened on that horrible Monday morning in the Comox hospital.

During the operation Dr. Woolrich found the femoral artery in Ivy's right groin and put it to one side. But he couldn't find the

the large saphenous vein. Somehow the artery collapsed and slipped off the retractor. The doctor mistook it for the vein. He tied it off. He cut it. He tried to pull it.

How or when he realized it was her artery, we'll never know.

I'm not hip on lawyers' legal jargon, but I know we issued a writ. We were going to sue.

The web grew more complicated every day. There were lawyers for St. Joseph Hospital, and for the Medical Protective Association, who were looking after the doctor. Our lawyer had to have a doctor for an expert witness.

I went to the fiery-tempered Dr. Smith . He knew all about the case and would help us, so I thought. But twice he put me off.

I approached him for the third time. "We can't find a doctor for a witness. Why won't you do it?"

"I've told you — everything I know is in writing. It's all there in black and white."

I had all the runs around I could stand. "Tell me, Doctor, why is the protection of your colleagues more important than your obligation to your patient?"

He began to bristle. Then he calmed and said, "I never thought of it quite that way."

In the end, a Vancouver doctor agreed to be our witness, but he never did have to appear. In the examination for discovery Dr. Woolrich admitted he hadn't given Ivy a pre-operative examination. Nor had he checked his files for her medical history. If he had, he'd have known why he couldn't find the vein in Ivy's right groin.

He'd removed it — eight years before.

We settled out of court. Our lawyer fees were three times as much as the doctor's fees. Dr. Smith attended Ivy for nearly four months; our lawyer didn't spend four days. When we saw Dr. Smith for the last time and thanked him for all he had done, he asked about fees, and he echoed my feelings when he shouted, "The sons of bitches."

Ivy went back to teaching kindergarten. She learned to drive her car, to dance, and to walk with grace and dignity. Her hospital dreams of new clothes were thwarted by short-styled skirts. Her prothesis limited her to one style of low-heeled shoes. Long trips in planes, trains and buses were uncomfortable and sometimes painful. Women's styles changed and slacks became a blessing.

Twenty-three years ago Ivy got her brand new leg and she still walks tall. A few wrinkles grace her lovely smile. Ten grandchildren have replaced the kindergarten and she loves and fusses over them all.

THE NIGHT I SPENT IN JAIL

If I had a choice of jails I don't suppose I'd have picked Nanaimo's. Especially on a Saturday night — the night before the Bath Tub Race.

Things had been difficult at home. Most married couples have times when they should be alone. I came home one day to find scrawled across our note pad, "I've gone. Don't try to find me."

When she didn't show for three nights running I realized she wasn't fooling and I started to track her down.

It wasn't difficult. She was staying with a friend in Nanaimo. But she wouldn't see me or talk to me. I was lonely and I missed her.

I tried the Legion, and it was just as lonely there. I knew I'd had one too many, but about ten p.m. I took off for Nanaimo.

The address was in a subdivision with street names from Robin Hood. It was past midnight and I had a hell of a time finding Sherwood Street — a cul de sac off Little John Avenue.

The house was in darkness, but my wife's car was parked in the driveway. I rang the doorbell. Her friend stepped onto the up-stairs balcony. "I'd like to see Ivy," I called up.

"Ivy doesn't want to see you, Gordon. Not tonight. Why don't you come back in the morning? It's almost two o'clock."

"Okay, I'll do that. What time's breakfast?"

"Phone in the morning. Good night!" and Juliet left the balcony.

The Island Highway runs through the middle of Nanaimo, and it's lined with motels, but "No Vacancy" blinked at every one I could see. Nanaimo's old coal-town area boasts twenty small hotels, each with a pub and a couple of rooms to make them legal. They were all full. So I went back to Sherwood Street to ask if I could sleep there.

I rattled the door but could get no answer, so I decided to sleep in my car. I'd just dozed off when a rap on the window woke me, and there in his peaked hat and uniform stood the law.

"What are you doing here?" he politely asked.

"My wife's in that house and she won't let me in, so I'm sleeping here. They asked me for breakfast."

"They complained that you're being a nuisance."

"I just want to see my wife. I don't think that's unreasonable."

"I'll see what she says."

He was gone a goodly time and when he came back he said, "I think you'd better come with me."

"Okay," I said, thinking as I got into the front seat of the patrol car that he must know a motel with a vacancy. "I couldn't find a motel room anywhere. Where are you taking me?"

"To the station. The police station."

"To the *police station*! What have *I* done?"

"You haven't done anything. It's what you *might* do."

"I'm not impaired."

"I don't think you'd pass a breathalyzer test! Besides, your wife doesn't want you sleeping in the car."

"Are you going to put me in jail?"

"We'll see."

He led me to a desk, a waist-high counter with a nervous clerk behind it and two policemen on my side. They all stood back as if I was about to attack them. They took my shoes, my belt, my wrist watch. They emptied all my pockets. They made a list of all my stuff and I signed it.

In my stocking feet and shirt and drooping pants they led me to a cell, clanged the steel barred door and locked me in.

My God! I'm in jail. How am I going get out? And when?

It was cold. I was alone—maybe I was in solitary. But the noise rocked and roared. The jail was packed with every raving drunk and drug addict on Vancouver Island—a deafening, frightening racket, as they screamed and cursed and cried.

A bright, naked light glowed against the ceiling. There was a three-foot shelf against the wall to sit and sleep on, a toilet without a seat; a sink without a hot water tap. I was cold and shivering. The guy from the desk came and looked in my cell and I begged him for a blanket.

"You're not allowed a blanket, but I'll see what I can do."

I get my blanket. The shelf is hard and cold. Some poor guy nearby screams and yells in terror. Then he begins to sob and say "Hail Marys". *I know I'll never sleep.*

Have I been in jail an hour? Or maybe two? It could be almost four a.m. It's daylight by four-thirty. Helluva lot of good that will do, with no windows. I wonder how long they'll keep me? Will I have to wait till Monday and appear in court? Will they charge me? What about that phone call the TV criminals always get?

One kook must be on drug withdrawal and finally yells himself to sleep. It's almost quiet now — the time of day people die. Just before the dawn ...

A guard or custodian comes to see if I'm still alive, at least he looks my way. "What's the time?" I ask.

"Doesn't matter son. You're not going anywhere."

The sadistic bastard could surely spare the time.

I've got a goddamn headache, feels like it's going to split. I bathe my face in cold water and drink gallons to quench my thirst. It must be getting close to breakfast, but there's neither sign nor smell of food.

I worry. The damn place is depressing. No one has been near me since they clanged the bloody door. Surely they'll have to feed me if they keep me all week end?

Then I get to thinking ... my wife must have put me here. But I'm lucky they didn't give me a breathalyzer or I might be here a week or more.

I hear a church bell toll, but it really doesn't help. Could be any time between eight and ten o'clock. At least some people have had breakfast and are off to early Mass. So maybe it's only six o'clock. I grab the bars and shake them and get an echo back. I haven't seen or heard a soul for days, it seems.

Then I hear a train whistle not so very far away. *By god! That's the E & N dayliner on its way to Courtenay.* I know it hits Courtenay at twelve-thirty or there-abouts. So it's around eleven Sunday morning.

How much longer have I got in this bloody place? Monday's sure a long way off.

So I settle back to wait. The train comes back about two so I'll have another time check before the day is done.

I fall asleep, I guess, for there's someone rattling my bars and the door clanks open. *Don't tell me they're going to set me free!*

Family

They did. They gave me back my shoes, and I pulled up my pants and belted them once again. There was no bill at their motel and they let me call a cab. I found my car. But not my wife. I made my journey home alone.

Some nights even now I stand again behind those bars, and shake them till I wake.

I'll never quite forget the only night I ever spent in jail.

From My Window

Survey Notes

Keith Wagner surveying E & N Boundary at Buttle Lake

From My Window

GILEAN'S CHANNEL ROCK

It was crow time. Each year the crows nest in the maple tree shading our survey office. The hungry youngsters caw from dawn to dusk, dulling the traffic noise from Courtenay's busy Cliffe Avenue.

The open door and windows welcomed the cool air of a sunny June morning. It was too fine a day to be stuck inside but the plan I was drafting had to be ready by noon.

"Where's the surveyor?" demanded a voice with a California accent. "Is he in?"

"Mr. Wagner will be with you in a minute," my secretary replied.

"Good morning," I said as I walked to the counter. "Can I help you?"

"Yaaa. Masters's the name. Tom Masters, attorney; this is my sister, Eileen Murphy. We're from L.A. We've bought one hundred and twenty-three acres with a half mile of waterfront on Cortes Island. A real steal. The owner wants to keep ten acres around the house and garden. George Silke sent us. Said you'd know what to do. Got sort of a map here."

His sport jacket, colour-coordinated slacks shirt and diamond-pinned tie looked snappy. He talked snappy. He oozed courtroom efficiency.

His sister wore a chic gabardine suit and a silk blouse anchored by a diamond-studded brooch. Her fingers showcased diamonds and gold. They both looked and smelled like brand new thousand-dollar bills.

Masters fumbled in his pocket and produced a wrinkled scrap of paper, part of a marine chart. "The land's down at the south end of the island. The ink dot is where the house is."

"I've a composite map of Cortes. I'll get it." I spread my map across the counter. "What's the legal description?"

"Let's see. It's here on the Interim Agreement. Er, yah — it's the Fractional SE 1/4 of Section 21."

"This must be the piece."

"Yep. The house is close to the shoreline. Garden's back a hundred feet. I've arranged for a plane to fly us in. Can we go this morning?"

This guy wants everything done yesterday. "I can't make it today. Maybe tomorrow."

"Silke says there's nothing to the survey. Might take a couple hours. I can have the plane at the Comox wharf in half an hour."

"No way we could do the survey in a couple of hours. And if we could it wouldn't help. All surveys must be approved by the Department of Highways before they can be registered in the Land Titles Office. Since the only access to this property is from the sea, the approval could take up to six weeks."

"Eileen's got a friend in Victoria, works for the government. I'll get him to help us. What's that fella's name, Sis?"

"I'm not sure," she replied. "I think it starts with a 'W'. Walls? Yah, John Walls. Distant cousin of my son David."

"I really don't think he'll be much help. I'll make a xerox of my map and you can take it to the local Highways office. You're driving aren't you?"

"Yah! That's her out there — the new Cadillac — an Eldorado. Biggest and best car in America! Cost me twenty grand. Gotta be careful where I park so she won't get scratched." I could see the long sleek car parked on the side street. She was snappy too.

I gave them a copy of my map and shipped them off to the local Highways office. I went back to my drafting table. The young crows cawed their endless lament. Maybe I'd better escape to Cortes.

After lunch, the Masters's were waiting for me.

"We talked to Highways and got these forms. Butler said you'd be familiar with them. Can we go this afternoon?"

"How about first thing tomorrow morning?"

"I'd like to get back to L.A. But I'm not too happy with the Interim Agreement; I want to go to Cortes and tape the conversation we'll have with her."

"Did you say **her**? Is the owner a woman?"

"Yah. Name's Gilean Douglas. Lives alone. George tells me she's a writer. We'll go get some lunch and I'll order a plane for two o'clock, okay?"

Well why not? It's a beautiful day. If he wants to pay for a flight to Cortes, I'd enjoy the ride and so would Keith. I can postpone my appointment.

"Okay, I'll be ready. I'll take a helper and some instruments."

"Fine. You want to go, Sis?"

"Why not? It's a beautiful day ... and remember it's my money we're spending!"

We met the Masters's at the Comox wharf, and thirty minutes later the Beaver was circling Channel Rock. A thousand feet below, tucked into a tiny cove, nestled a cottage, well protected from the southeasters and guarded by an island-sized rock. A trace of smoke beckoned from the chimney. At the tide line a row boat rested on a plank ways. A path pushed through a bank of flowers and headed for the far corner of the house, turned a soft right angle and divided the house from the woodshed.

To the north the lonely wooded shoreline zigzagged to the blue horizon. To the south the rocky beach pulled a peninsula into the Gulf of Georgia. A tree-haired ridge backboned the peninsula to the island. Over and beyond the peninsula, in a lake-like bay, a wharf nursed three fishing boats and a packer's barge. Half a dozen houses fought for space around the wharf head.

Our pilot side-slipped the Beaver to a gentle landing and we floated in to the rocky beach. We walked up the foot- smoothed path, and as we turned the corner a woman emerged from the forest. A yellow bandanna tamed her hair, and the blue of the scarf wrapped high around her throat enhanced the colour of her eyes. She wore a checkered shirt, faded jeans lightly powdered with fresh soil, and carried a trowel. She looked puzzled as we gathered around her back door. "Oh! It's you, Mr. Masters. This is a surprise!"

"This is Gordon Wagner and his son Keith, land surveyors from Courtenay. You've met my sister. We're here to define the area you want to exclude from the sale."

I studied our obviously reluctant host. She lived here alone; the nearest neighbor was a mile or more away. The well- tended yard, the neatly stacked wood pile, the smiling flower beds, all whispered tenderness and care. A womanly ruggedness shone from her face, and toned the polished hoarseness of her voice. She belonged to Channel Rock.

"Yes," she sighed. "I want to keep the house, of course. And the garden, the cottage, and the well. Go far enough north to protect Channel Rock's cove, and far enough south to keep the cottage and its cove. What's the size of ten acres?"

"A ten-acre square is 660 feet by 660 feet." I said. "Let's walk around and see where things are, and take some measurements."

Gilean led us to the garden, a half-acre patch of ground she'd wrestled from the rain forest, and showed us the irrigation system she'd rigged. After taking us to the cottage, she started up a trail.

Then she stopped. "I **must** retain the right to use this trail. It's my access to the old Indian pictographs. The Indian medicine men came here for the equinox. One aged painting is on a rock face at right angles to the sun at high noon. From there they could see the sun rise and set. It is a cherished treasure and I visit it every spring and fall."

"I hope we're going to end up with a parcel more or less rectangular. If we have to jog the boundaries to take in all these places, we'll have an odd looking lot," grumbled Masters. "What do you think, Sis?"

"Well, I thought the idea was to have a regular lot — just like a city lot, only bigger," said Mrs. Murphy. "I don't care much about Indian picture grafs or whatever you call them."

"Let's wait until we get something on paper," I said. "What else is there, Mrs. Douglas?"

"We'll go back toward the house and I'll show you the trail to Whaletown, and where I want the north boundary."

As we passed the house Mrs. Murphy said, "I think I'll stay here. I've seen all I want to see of *this* place."

Gilean disregarded her comment, and said. "There are lawn chairs by the house and the view is magnificent. Just make yourself at home."

The trail to Whaletown led up the ridge. "I go for my mail twice a week. It's only three miles. A lovely walk and good exercise. When I need supplies I take the boat, if it isn't stormy. If it's rough I walk and carry back what I need," Gilean explained, "and here is my look out." She pointed to an axe-hewn bench just off the trail.

To the west an island-like rock and over-hanging cedar boughs framed the view. Quadra Island sprang from the blue waters of the Gulf — an arch of green, scalloped by Vancouver Island's snow-capped mountains. Thunderclouds tumbled around the mountain tops.

"I want the north boundary to clear the bench by at least 100 feet and to have all of Channel Rock's cove well within my lot."

"How far are we from the house, Keith?" I asked.

"Almost 400 feet. There'll be about 750 of waterfront." He paused to take a compass reading. "An east-west line is well clear of your Channel Rock cove, Mrs. Douglas."

"Fine," she replied. "Mr. Masters knows I want the boundary here."

"Yes, Mrs. Douglas, But I didn't think you'd be keeping 750 feet of waterfront."

I could feel trouble. "I think we have all the information we need. Why don't you two go back to the house, while Keith and I get something on paper?"

When we returned to the house I showed them our sketch plan. "I'll prepare a proper plan and get it to Highways tomorrow — but we'll be lucky if we get an answer in six weeks."

Masters' sister flashed her diamonds and her snappy black eyes. "Tom tells me your lot will take 750 feet of waterfront. I thought you said 660 feet was ten acres. We want to keep as much waterfront as possible. After all, we want as many waterfront lots as we can get, and 750 feet would be ten city lots."

"Waterfront lots!" gasped Gilean. I watched her face pale. "You never mentioned city lots before. You said you were going to keep it just the way it was."

"We'll have to wait and see what Highways' requirements are," I cut in. "Do I hear a plane?"

"Looks like our Beaver, Dad," said Keith.

As I said goodbye I saw tears drop from Gilean's deep blue eyes and sadness scroll across her face.

Back in the office, Masters continued to push. "I want you to give this top priority. We're heading back to L.A. in the morning, but you've got my card. I'll leave money with Silke for your account. Come on, Eileen. Let's get back to the hotel. I need a double Scotch."

"Great idea!" she chimed. "I've got a funny feeling about this whole deal. I was getting bad vibes from that Douglas woman."

I walked them to their glimmering Eldorado and watched the California license fade down the street, wondering about vibes. I locked the office door. The crows still cawed.

The next day I took the proposed plan to Highways. Mike said the local office would recommend it, but Victoria might require some road dedication. We'd just have to wait.

Ten days later, about four on a Friday afternoon, Masters phoned from California. "You heard anything from Highways ?"

"Not yet."

"What the hell's the holdup?"

"You'll just have to be patient. There's nothing I can do to hurry Highways."

"Can't you spread a little moolah around? Maybe a case of Scotch would help."

"I don't operate that way. I'll let you know as soon as I hear ... Yes, Mr. Masters. I understand. Goodbye now."

The next week he sent a letter urging me to expedite the approval.

The following week another phone call—and again about four p.m. Keith took the call.

"You heard anything from Highways?" I could hear the slurred voice booming out of the phone from across the room.

"No word yet Mr. Masters."

"Tell those S.O.B.'s at Highways to get off their fat asses or I'll put a bomb under 'em!"

"Take it easy, Mr. Masters." Keith replied.

"**You're** the ones taking it easy! If you don't get the lead out, I'll get another surveyor. My attorney in Victoria says **his** surveyor could do the survey tomorrow."

"Fine, Mr. Masters. You do whatever you think best." Keith hung up. "The guy's drunk, Dad."

"Seems to get into his cups every Friday afternoon."

A week later I was in Victoria. I'd had a hectic day, and was enjoying a cup of coffee in the Dominion Hotel, when I was called to the phone in the lobby. It was Masters. Somehow he'd found me.

His speech was thick and we had a poor connection. I had to shout to make him hear. The lobby was full of long-eared people.

But I couldn't shake him. He was tanked and tenacious. And I was embarrassed and exasperated, so I hung up.

Another letter and two phone calls later Highways gave their approval. It was late July. The young crows had grown wings and spent the long days pleading for food.

I phoned George Silke, "We've received approval for the Douglas/Masters survey on Cortes. Could you call Masters and tell him? He's pestered the dickens out of me."

"Sure, I'll phone him. When are you going to do the survey?"

"We'll fly over early Monday morning. George... Masters said he'd left funds with you to pay my survey account. Thought I'd check before we start the work."

"He didn't leave any money with me."

"You must hold the down payment for the Agreement — It's an $85,000 deal, isn't it?"

"All I have is $1.00."

"What? Well, when you phone ask him to get some money up here. Meantime, I'll go ahead with the survey."

"I'll tell him. Let me know how things go."

I hung up. I felt those 'vibes' again. They weren't good.

In late July it's difficult to find a place to stay on Cortes. But Harold and Dolly Hansen agreed to give us a room and feed us. Son Jeff would boat the crew to work. We flew into Channel Rock early Monday morning.

Gilean was on the beach to greet us. The calm sea, the cloudless sky, and the eight-thirty heat of the sun promised a hot and dry forest. We unloaded the gear and discussed the details of the survey. Then Keith and his helpers left to find the north boundary and get started. I turned back to the plane.

Gilean stopped me. "Mr. Wagner, could I have a word with you before you go?"

"Certainly." I followed her into the house and sank into a chair by her front room window.

What a peaceful place, I thought, admiring the view of Uganda Pass framed by Channel Rock, with her flowers in the foreground.

I heard a sniffle. Gilean was crying. "What have I done, Gordon?" She sobbed, "I don't want to sell any part of Channel Rock. For three years I've been working under a small grant to write a book. It requires a great deal of research, which leaves me no time to earn money with other writing. I keep my expenses to a minimum, and the garden helps, but food is high here. My savings are almost gone, so I thought I might sell part of my one hundred and twenty-three acres. I've been just sick ever since you were here. I wish I'd never seen Masters, or Silke or any of them."

She dried her eyes and in a sob-strained voice whispered, "I can't imagine what possessed me. What can I do?"

"Don't be upset." I soothed her. "I've had a queer feeling about this deal from the beginning, and Masters has given me a rough time. He told me he'd left money with George Silke for the survey, but he didn't. Do you have a copy of your agreement?"

"I've the paper George Silke left me. Is this it?"

I read the Agreement. The price was $85,000 and it acknowledged the receipt of $1.00 with all the obligations and their cost for Gilean.

"A rather tall order for $1.00." I said. "I'm a Notary Public, and I don't think this is a valid contract. Masters could sue for specific performance, and if it goes to court you never know what a judge will rule. But I don't think you have to complete the sale."

Her moist eyes gleamed with hope. "Do you really think so? Are you sure?"

"Let me check with a lawyer friend. You're on the Campbell River exchange? I'll give Ray a call right now."

I watched her face coming back to life as I talked to him. And when I said, "He agrees with me", she squeezed my hand in both of hers, and for a moment I thought she was going to kiss me.

"How can I ever thank you?"

"It's part of my job. I'm sure everything will turn out all right, but since we've started the field work we should finish the survey. You might need it if Masters gets nasty. Besides, any time you get anything from Highways you should use it. Lord knows what they may require a year from now. And it'll be good to have a separate title to the house and the ten acres."

"Whatever you think best. I only hope we can save Channel Rock!"

I drafted the plan of the Channel Rock survey, sent the original to the Highways and a print to Masters, advising him that Mrs. Douglas would delay registration of the plan until he had placed the $85,000 in the trust account of his solicitor. I waited. The crows cawed.

Two mornings later, Masters was on the phone. "What in hell is going on up there? I'm not sending any goddamn $85,000 to any solicitor! You tell Mrs. Douglas to read her Agreement. And if she can't understand plain English, she'd better get a lawyer."

"I believe Mrs. Douglas is acting on the advice of her lawyer."

"Yeah? Well as far as I'm concerned we have a valid contract and I intend to enforce it. I'm going to bloody well tell my Victoria solicitor to issue a writ for specific performance. You can tell Mrs. Douglas."

"I'll do that."

When I called Gilean she said, "I was afraid he'd get nasty. What should I do?"

"Just sit tight. You've got the survey ready to register in the Land Titles Office. It's his move now. Don't worry about it. If you hear anything let me know."

"Yes, I will."

Two weeks later Gilean phoned. "I have just had a visit from the sheriff," her hoarse voice trembled. "Mrs. Murphy is asking for specific performance of our Interim Agreement. I'm really upset. What will I do? How did I ever get into such a mess?"

"Just take it easy. When is the next mail out of Cortes? I'd like to have a copy of the writ."

"I can get it into today's mail. I feel almost like a criminal. Maybe we should do whatever the Masters's want. I can't bear the thought of going to court."

"Try not to worry. I'm sure you'll never go to court. I'll keep in touch. Just keep writing and take care of beautiful Channel Rock."

John Wodden was the Masters' lawyer. I'd known John for years and I didn't hesitate to call him. I told him Mrs. Douglas had completed her part of the agreement. The survey was completed and ready for registration. "Mrs. Douglas doesn't want to create the new lot if the deal collapses." I explained.

"I didn't realize the plan was ready for deposit," he replied. "I'll advise Mrs. Murphy to have the funds put in my trust account. Then you can register your survey plan."

Two weeks passed. Not a sound from them.

Gilean called, "I don't like to bother you, but have you heard anything from Mr. Wodden or the Masters's?"

"Nothing yet."

"I just can't settle down. I haven't written anything for days. I'm just sick."

I could almost hear the tears drop. "I'll try to get John Wodden on the phone. I'll call you back."

"Hello John. Gordon Wagner here, Have you any news from the Masters?"

"I just finished dictating a letter to Mrs. Douglas. Masters' sister has decided to abandon the sale. He insists on a quit claim from Gilean Douglas, and relief from any obligation to you. I'll send the document to you. Have it signed and witnessed by both of you."

"Thank you John. You'll have it by return mail."

I phoned Gilean. As calmly as I could, I said, "Gilean we've won! The Masters's have withdrawn their offer."

There was a long pause.

"Gilean? Are you all right?"

Then I heard her sigh, "Oh! Thank God! I can't believe it's over. How can I ever thank you for saving Channel Rock?"

We not only saved Channel Rock, but I came to know Gilean Douglas, to read her books and to revel in her poetry. We served concurrent terms for the Regional District of Comox-Strathcona.

She published *The Protected Place*, the story of her love for Channel Rock, how she found it, how the Indians worshipped at the pictographs. She interlaced John Pool's love of solitude with his struggle to make Channel Rock his home, after the tragedy of World War One. She took us month by month through the birth of spring, the lush of summer, the demise of autumn, to the quiet rest of winter. Her words preserved the sights and sounds of Channel Rock and soothed the soul with beauty. I loved it. When she told me I was the Gordon in the dedication, I was honoured.

She still lives on Cortes Island, still walks to Whaletown for her mail. She'll protect Channel Rock and write about its treasures until the day she dies. Channel Rock is in good hands.

Years ago the maple tree and my office surrendered to the blacktop of a parking lot. But each June the cawing of young crows takes me back to memories of Channel Rock and a fine woman.

THE TELEPHONE LINE SURVEYOR

I limit myself to one visitor a week," said Gilean Douglas "I've had a visitor this week, and someone's coming next week. But the week after — how's Friday, the 9th of May?"

"Fine. I'll catch the nine o'clock ferry out of Heriot Bay and be at Channel Rock by eleven," I replied. She told me how to find and follow the mile-and-a-half path from Cortes Island's Whaletown Road to her home at Channel Rock. I sketched a map. I hadn't seen Gilean for years, not since we both served our days

106

on the Comox-Strathcona Regional Board. I was writing the story of how we saved Channel Rock from land developers. The yarn needed more of Gilean Douglas, so I was happy when my "week" arrived.

My brief case (packed with manuscripts, tape recorder, and two of Gilean's books for autographs), my camera and a bag of fresh vegetables, were in my truck. I headed for Campbell River and the early morning eight o'clock ferry to Quadra Island.

Four blocks from home I missed my candies. I'd left them on the kitchen counter. For years I've carried candy wherever I go. I seldom eat a midday meal, but I usually carry some paper-wrapped hard candies in my pocket.

You won't need them today, Gordon. Gilean asked what you'd like for lunch.

On Cortes Island, with the help of a friendly Islander, I found the entrance off the Whaletown Road to Gilean's path and parked my truck.

A wide trail started into the silent forest but soon narrowed to a single lane. No one had used the trail for months. Last fall's leaves still carpeted the forest floor, hiding the path. Several times I lost it and had to watch for pieces cut out of windfalls to get back on track.

I found the black phone wire across the path, the one Gilean had told me to watch for, found the "Y" and took the left path. It led on, uphill and downhill.

I knew from reading Gilean's *The Protected Place* I'd be near Channel Rock when I could see the water, and I'd go through the "dark place", a legendary area of the island filled with evil spirits affecting life in the forest and in the adjacent sea.

Again I lost the trail. I could see the water through the dark trees. And I could see a cove. Was it the cottage cove? Had I gone too far? The tide was low, so I walked out onto the beach. Ah — there was the roof of a house and a smoke-beckoning chimney; still half a mile to go. Back on the path, I followed it through the dark forest, stepping gingerly as the path skirted a cliff, and climbed the last incline – and there was Channel Rock.

The brown house with its green trim, the rocks robed in velvet moss, the May-fresh greens of the forest, and a bed of yellow tulips all canvassed on a cloud-fluffy blue sky and backed by white-capped waters of Uganda Passage, smiled, "Welcome".

The back door, joined to the woodshed by a short clothesline and guarded by a small table holding a still life arrangement of two water buckets, a dipper and a washbasin reminded me of Goldilock's cottage. I felt like one of the Three Bears.

I rang the rope of bells strung across the top of the door.

Time had been kind to Gilean, though she seemed smaller and more fragile. "Gilean, it's good to see you!" I offered my hand.

"No! No, I can't take your hand. My doctor was here yesterday and warned me that, because I live an isolated life here, I'm very vulnerable to other people's colds and flu. So would you please wash your hands in the basin? There's a little bleach in the water, and here's a towel." Then she handed me a small glass. "This is Listerine. Would you mind gargling your throat?"

When I finished my debugging, she took my hand. "It's wonderful to see you. Sorry I have to be so fussy."

"Oh, that's okay," I smiled. "I got your lettuce. Siefferts' market-garden opened yesterday. There's new spinach and cucumbers. Hope you like them?"

"Great! I haven't had either for ages, thank you. Now come in and make yourself comfortable."

We spent an enjoyable morning. She read my "Dyke House" story and liked it. But when she read "Gilean's Channel Rock", I had to take out the description of her straw hat and her coveralls. "I dress better than that for my garden and flowers!" she protested.

She insisted I delete all references to age and time. "I've always been young to my readers and I intend to stay young."

Gilean poured sherry and we toasted the success of our story. Then she served soup, fresh-baked apple pie, and good coffee, all with bone china, fine crystal and sterling silver. I felt honoured.

She led me to her garden, a half acre, protected on the east and north by high rocky hills, crowded on the west by the creeping rain forest, and open on the south to the sun and sea. As we walked through her fairy-land, I recognized the big trees, the root house, the cottage and the barn she describes in *The Protected Place*. I felt at home.

"It's five o'clock," she warned. "Time to leave. The last ferry sails at five-fifty."

At the door I held her hand, "Goodbye, thanks for the lunch. Wonderful to see you again. I did enjoy myself."

"Thank you. Thank you for coming. And this time, I am **going** to kiss you!" And she did.

I checked the angle of the sun to get my directions and headed up the trail for Whaletown. It had taken me thirty minutes to walk in. There was no need to hurry.

Ten minutes later, again near the "dark place" I lost the path. I spotted a black phone line lying near my feet. It was the same as the one I'd seen at the "Y".

Follow this, Gordon. It'll lead back to the path.

It headed up hill towards an opening. I followed it for a couple of hundred feet. It should turn left soon. I grabbed the wire and gave it a pull. It still snaked uphill.

Go a little further, Gordon. It looks good ahead.

I went another 100 feet. The hill was getting steeper, the brief case heavier, and the camera was a damn nuisance. I stopped to catch my breath.

This damn wire has to lead to the Whaletown Road. We're in open country; it's got to turn soon. Keep going, Gordon.

I struggled up hill. I rested and looked around, and I gave the wire another pull. Up the hill it went. I could see the top.

To my right, through the open forest, I could see another rocky hill. To my left, against the low afternoon sun, yet another rocky hill outlined the horizon.

Dammit, Gordon, you've boxed yourself in. The bloody phone line goes over the top of the mountain, and you've only got 30 minutes. If you go back and have trouble finding Gilean's trail in the "dark" trees, you'll miss the ferry. It's not far to the top and it'll be all down hill from there. Get going.

The hill got tougher. I had to stop every 100 feet to catch my breath, and I couldn't rest long enough to recover my strength.

You'll make the top this time. It can't be more than 75 feet.

I broke over the crest.

Goddam, it's still 200 feet! But not as steep. You need a candy.

I knew it was useless but I searched my pockets. Two crumpled wrappers -- no candy.

I dragged myself, the brief case and the camera to the top. I could see the road, and a house, about a quarter mile away and 400 feet below.

You can make it now. You've still got 26 minutes. But get going boy. No time to spare.

For about 200 feet it was easy going. Then I came to a tree — with the damn phone line tied around it and dangling down a perpendicular cliff.

Good God, Gordon! It must be 70 or 80 feet to the bottom. You'll have to find a way around it... or spend the night on Cortes.

I couldn't go to the left. The vertical face extended as far as I could see. There were ledges to my right, but I didn't want to start down and have to turn back.

I searched for a deer trail. Deer know every path over every cliff. But there were no deer signs.

You stupid bastard. You not only came without candy, you don't have a knife or a match! What if you fall and break a leg? It's a hell of a long way to drag yourself to the road. Nobody'll ever hear you.

110

I zipped my camera inside my jacket, put the brief case in my left hand, and started down. I eased myself down to the first ledge, stepped to the second then the third.

The next one, nearly four feet away, was less than a foot wide with a sturdy spiraea growing on it. But I could see the ledge beyond, and it was wider.

Okay, Wagner—but watch it. It's still 50 feet to the bottom.

I grabbed the spiraea. Swung across. Paused. Stepped to the next ledge.

Ten feet from the bottom I sat on my behind and slid the rest of the way into a cushion of salal.

The phone line dangled down the cliff and disappeared into the underbrush. I fought and dragged myself and my brief case through the clawing salal. It thickened. I tired. The phone line broke out of the salal across a small creek.

A cool drink helped, and I scrambled up the bank into the tangled branches of a spruce windfall. I tripped and the bloody spruce threw me back into the creek.

You son of a bitch! To hell with you. I'll head for the beach.

I fought through the underbrush and slithered down onto the beach. I had seventeen minutes left.

A road from the beach passed a house, but it looked vacant. There was no car; I **had** to have a car. I needed a ride to win.

I tried to hurry. Even on the level road I tired. When I hit the hill I was stopping every 50 feet. My feet stumbled in the gravel. I was exhausted.

Around a turn I saw the pavement and forced myself over the last 100 feet. I dropped the briefcase and the camera in the road-side grass and headed for my truck.

But I could hardly put one foot ahead of the other, and it was all uphill.

You'll never make it, Gordon. Might as well sit down and rest...no, by God! There's a truck coming! Now, make damn sure you stop him.

I straddled the middle of road, arms stretched wide. The truck slowed and stopped. I opened the door and fell across the seat. "Take me to my truck," I gasped. "My truck — up the road."

"Pull your feet in and shut the door," ordered the startled driver.

"I've walked out from Gilean Douglas' place. Got following a phone line. Came right over the damn mountain. I gotta catch that last ferry. I'll just make it, thanks to you."

He dropped me near my truck. I thanked him, drove back to pick up the brief case and camera, and arrived at the ferry as they started to load.

Wagner, you're lucky. You could be lying at the bottom of that cliff. Next time you walk into Channel Rock do what your father told you! "Gordon, always have some money, some matches and a jackknife in your pocket. And don't forget some candies."

Yes, Dad. And I'll stay away from telephone lines too.

Levack Mine

LEVACK'S NARROW MINE

The dirty thirties had driven me to the International Nickel Company's town of Levack. I'd spent all my life in the openness of Saskatchewan's prairies. Working in the nickel mines at Levack narrowed my world.

The town sits in a narrow clearing in a narrow valley in northern Ontario. Long narrow bunk-houses line one side of the tracks; across the tracks tattle-tale-gray frame-houses squat along narrow lanes. Up the tracks the narrow headframe of the mines pierces the cloud-cramped skyline.

Dimly-lit halls run down the narrow bunk-houses; shrunken doors open into compressed rooms; two single beds and two small dressers squeeze between the concrete walls; two compact closets huddle in their separate corners. In a long dining hall, with slim tables, flanked by long skinny benches, the cooks serve

113

flat-tasting meals in a restricted social atmosphere. We sit down. We eat. We get up. We get out.

At the mine, the change house has long rows of slender lockers — double lockers, one up, one down. The 'up' one is for street clothes, the 'down' one for dry sweat-soaked underwear, socks and jeans. We never wash our work clothes: we replace them every two weeks, every payday. Fine coal-black dust saturates the fabric; after two weeks the board-stiff underwear stands unassisted, ready to rasp the skin breaking the clothing to fit as we climb into it.

My days are lightless. In the winter it's still dark at seven a.m. The plunging skip whips me down the steep inclined shaft 2000 feet into the black bowels of the mine. Eight hours later I'm coughed back to surface. It's dark again. I work six days without seeing daylight.

Underground, rock-walled tunnels grooved by narrow-gauged rails lead to smaller tunnels. The air in them is narrow. Each day huge pumps compress more tons of air into the mine than tons of ore are hoisted to the surface by whizzing buckets. It's dark in the hole. The fork-tongued flames of the carbide lamps cast a spooky glow. The weak light struggles against the forbidding wall of the dark. The weight of the heavy hard-hat holding the carbide lamp presses me against the rock floor. My partner's light snakes through the dark like the dancing head of a cobra.

We blast with dynamite a hunk of ore too big to smash with the ten-pound sledge hammer. The stope boss clears the area, guards the entrance, lights the fuse runs and yells, "Fire!" We wait. B-A-N-G! The swooshing air blasts down the tunnel. The carbide light dies. The darkness is absolute. Only if you lose both eyes will it be that dark again. The darkness narrows to an infinity unlit by stars.

In the bunk-house at night I listen to my short-wave radio. Or I take a trip up a one-way road to a tarpapered shack. In the kerosene-lighted, smoke-filled house I can get a narrow- necked bottle of beer for two-bits, or a short shot of rye for a quarter, or for two bucks I can join the lineup at the bottom of the stairs.

Long after I leave Levack, nightmares follow me. I am trapped in a shrinking pocket. The space atop the pile of muck is too narrow to squeeze through. The piled-up slabs of ore are too heavy to move, too thick to break. I narrow myself for one last squeeze. I lose my light. I grab. I wake clawing at the bedclothes, drenched in sweat. There's light, thank God! Don't let me die in the narrow dark.

THE LITTLE HOUSE ON THE DYKE ROAD

Remember me? I'm the little shack that used to live on the Dyke Road. (I know it's called the Comox Road now but when I was growing up it was the Dyke Road.) I always think of myself as the "The Little Old House on the Dyke Road."

I can't remember how old I am. Obbie Bell says my shingled sides had grayed and I had moss in my hair 'way back in '25. He helped his dad build Sam McLeod's sawmill. They built it right across the road from me — across the Dyke Road and along side Sam's shingle mill. So I guess I'm in my mid-sixties.

I'm not much good at dates, but I can remember being put together. I'm not very big, you know — just 12 feet wide and 16 feet long. Sam brought shiny new shingles from the mill at Fanny Bay to cover my naked shiplap sides. Abe Orr and Pappy Edwards' Hardware sold him a fine paneled door and three paned windows. Pete Godfrey came from Cumberland to build my chimney.

O'course they started with my legs. They're almost 12 feet long, and buried 4 feet in the mud of Matthewson's slough.

I was sure proud of my legs. Sam meant me to be around for awhile, so he had Jack McQuinn pick out four silky peeled-cedar poles from K.& K.'s Camp 3 pole yard. Real beauties. Had 'em brought down on the train. Jack Carthew hauled 'em from the Riverside Hotel with his team of grays.

I mind the day they plumbed and braced them. Bert Marriott said, "Them's the finest set of legs I've ever seen this side of Cordova Street." Same size top and bottom. No knots. And the seams straight as a dye.

Painted by Sandy Heybroek

Small as I was, Sam gave me light and water. Happy Williams connected me to the water line — the line Courtenay said they'd "lent" the folks of Comox. Young Bill McKee hooked me up to the 25-cycle power that Clinton Woods bought from the Canadian Collieries and peddled up and down the Valley — the only 25 cycle current in North America.

I was finished just before Easter. My, I did feel fresh and fine that Easter morning! I'd have joined the Easter Parade if I could have got my long legs to move.

Easter must have been mid-April that year, 'cause my friend Gracie was in full bloom. Gracie's a wild apple tree. She was fifteen when I arrived. Sam's men were careful not to hurt her while they were puttin' me together.

Gracie was in petal-pink that Easter morning, and we did look pretty side by side, with the calm slough all around us and a new coat of green on Smith's pasture.

I remember Sam Mcleod's family, that first Easter. They must've come straight from church — 'least they came from up the river. They were all decked out in their Sunday best, and Sam's Tin Lizzie shone like black patent leather. Sam unlocked my door and they all crowded in. I can still feel their fingers caressing the smoothness of my No. 1 clear-cedar shiplap walls, their eyes admiring my paneled windows, and the electric light dangling from the ceiling and the water pipe against the wall.

"Oh, Pa, what a perfect playhouse!" Annie said. "Will you build us one like this at home?"

"Maybe some day Annie, but not this year," replied Sam.

"Hey, Pa, can Hib and me camp here tonight?" asked eight-year-old Ray. "We could get some early morning trout off the boom. How about it. Pa?"

"You boys aren't gonna sleep in this two by four shack. Your Pa'll have you working in the mill soon enough," announced Mrs. McLeod. "Come on, Sam, let's get these kids home before they get any more wild ideas. Besides, your Chinese watchman's moving in tomorrow. What's his name?"

"Johnny Mah Chee. He's been with us ever since the shingle mill was started."

So for a couple of years I was part Chinese. I loved John Mah Chee. He built a high page-wire fence all around me so Smith's cows couldn't rub against my graceful legs. He planted a garden. And he made a flower bed around Gracie's trunk so she wouldn't feel so bad when she lost the petals off her Easter bonnet. Johnny kept those flowers blooming till Gracie's sour apples turned to autumn red.

Then one day Johnny didn't come back. Some people came and took his pretty silk lady off the wall. They talked Chinese so I didn't know for days about Johnny getting killed. That was the first time I cried.

I was alone for a while after Johnny left, until one day a young couple came to look at me.

"It's awfully small, Mel," said Alma (Lafond) Smith.

"But Sam McLeod says we can live here for $5 a month. What do you think, love?"

"Melville C. Smith, if you're here, you know I'll be happy! I'll make it cozy. I'll scrub her good, and make some pretty curtains for the windows, and maybe we can find some paint."

So I got a real good cleaning and fresh paint on my walls. They divided me in two, 'cause Alma said there was no way she would eat and sleep in the same room. "And I'm not climbing up and down a ladder to the outhouse," she added. So they attached a four by four privy to my back wall and installed a Johnson bar. The tide flushed it twice a day. Mel claimed I was the first house on the Dyke Road to have a flush toilet.

Alma said I had to wear a skirt, too. So they shiplapped and shingled me to the ground and hid my pretty cedar legs. She frilled my windows with lacy curtains, scrubbed my edge-grained fir floor to sandy whiteness, hung dainty pictures on my walls, and kept fresh flowers on the table. I was a real lady!

Those were happy days. I never knew two people could be so kind to one another. They loved in a quiet simple way, and shared their love. I never heard an angry word.

One day Mel said he'd found a bigger house and maybe they should move. Alma agreed, but she hated to leave. "I'll miss my Tom Thumb house," she sighed.

I was lonely when they left. That was the second time I cried.

'Twas '26 or maybe '27 when Sam brought Alex Herd to stay. Nice enough fellah — but hated washing dishes. He fried most of his food and ate it out of the frying pan. What he didn't eat for dinner he had for supper. If he ate it all he washed the frying pan. My goodness, I did get greasy!

But he was a friendly guy, and liked lots of company. I remember the young fellows would gather at lunch time and after work. Some of them are still around. You likely know them. There was Obbie Bell, who helped build the mill, he was a sawyer. Floyd Clearly and Mel (Smitty) Smith worked the boom. There was Allan Dingwall, Harold Watkinson, E.L. Thompson and Joe Thomson. Dick Grimes, Angus Hamilton and of course, Alex Herd. I remember Fletcher, he built boats in a shop nearby. Bert Marriott trucked lumber around the valley. So did the Creech boys — Tom, Dick and Harry.

Those were busy years with Sam McLeod and his partner McDonald, the sawmill and the shingle mill going full blast. Times were good and everybody was working.

Then in '31 the depression shut down both mills and I lived alone for several years. Sam wasn't too well. And when World War II came there was no money for sawmills and no men to run them. I spent most of those years sheltering mice and swallows.

Sam's sons, Ray and Hibberd, returned from the war, and in '47 reopened the sawmill. Charlie Widen sharpened the saws. He needed to be close to the mill, so he rented me for $10 a month. He cleaned and tiddled me up real nice-like for a bachelor man. Fixed a saw vice alongside me.

Charlie was an expert. In the days of cross-cut saws a good filer was a faller's best friend. I don't know how he did it with just one eye.

When the mill burnt down in '53, Charlie bought me from Sam McLeod. Paid $500 for me. Then the power saws killed Charlie's filing business. He couldn't manage on his pension, so he sold a half interest in me to his Finnish friend, Leo Rosenlof. Leo had also lost an eye. I had few dull moments once these one-eyed loggers settled in!

Charlie left first. He sold his half to Leo. They took Charlie to a logger's rest home in Nanaimo to file his last days away.

Next thing I knew, Leo sold me to the National Second Century Fund for $5000. Imagine me being worth so much. It surprised Leo too. They said he could live there for the rest of his life. I wonder why they paid so much for me ... But I didn't worry. By then my outside shingles had weathered to soft silver. And Leo took good care of me. Kept me neat and clean inside.

One morning Leo didn't get up. I knew he was dead but there was nothing I could do. I watched as he was carried away. Now I was alone again. All alone. I shed a tear for Leo – and waited.

One day some people came and took all Leo's things away. I felt as if my guts were ripped apart. Someone cut a hole in my blind end-wall and fixed it like a shutter. "To watch the birds," I heard them say.

It took me a long time to put it all together, but I think I've got it now. The National Second Century Fund bought me to help save their friends, the birds. Johnny, Mel and Alma, Charlie, Leo and I had fed the birds for years. Well, I couldn't do it by myself. So they arranged to have the Comox-Strathcona Natural History Society look after me and guard our precious slough.

It's Easter, 1986. I've always felt that Easter was my birthday. This year Easter Sunday was warm and sunny – just like the day the McLeod family visited me so many years ago. But Gracie hasn't got her petal-pink bonnet on yet. Easter's early this year.

It's Easter Monday. The elderberry's leafing. Spring awakes the slough, I hear Tom Berry's cow grazing on the new grass next door. A new calf is bawling for its mother. The sun warms the shadows and clears the mist away. I recognize the swallows I nested just last year. What a lovely morning! What a day to be alive!

I'm having company. Sounds like my friendly bird watchers. They come in and I hear some one say, "There's nothing worth saving in here."

Next thing I know they're at the bottom of my cedar skirt and they're splashing something on my silvered shingles.

My God! It's stove oil. I know the smell. They're going to burn me ...

If there's a God for little houses, please stop them. **No! No! No! Not on Easter Monday! Not on my birthday!**

They light my southeast corner. My lovely cedar leg is burning. I start to spark and crackle, and I begin to roar. The heat lifts me skyward and I see my flaming home below. In peace, I spread myself across the valley and search for friends I know.

I cry for the last time.

JUNE'S NOVEMBER

November roars into June, jumbling Comox Bay, dousing lights and ruining weekend schedules.

The warm days of May's last week buried the lingering chills of winter in the snows of the Comox Glacier. But this morning a cake-like icing of late spring snow scallops the mountain tops. The early morning light reveals the emerald slopes of the rain forest, and the hills and valleys drape the mountain sides in rich robes of green velvet. Invisible planes, jetting to and from Japan, slice the sky with sharp vapour trails that soon widen into healing white clouds. Framed between Comox Spit's yellow broom and the snows of Mount Arrowsmith, the azure sky and the smooth cobalt waters of the bay meet the horizon. With the garden in, the roses blooming, the lawn trimmed, we and our starlings' youngsters prepare for summer's birthday just three weeks away.

But last night the earth's axis must have shifted, and a mad November pounces on our gem-like bay. A wild southeaster pushes white caps up the river, crochets the shore with white bands of foamy lace, and throws great gobs of froth at the neighbor's roses, smearing our windows.

Next door, a tough, wind-whipped hawthorn tree, trimmed high, and profiled like a human head, nods madly in the gale and mouth-like branches scream their agony at the loss of leaf and limb. A young tree, slim and tall, bows her leafy top and huddles like a wounded swan.

Two seagulls, in fine pitch and full throttle, dip and glide against the gale in a graceful exhibition of low flying. A crow emerges from between the houses, meets an updraft. Flips and almost hits the eaves. Stalls. Falls halfway to the ground. Steps on the gas. Flaps up his r.p.m.'s and disappears around the corner. A young starling leans into the wind, hangs onto the grass as he hunts his breakfast in the new-mown lawn. I tap the window. His stubby new-found wings get him airborne. He flies backwards and lands ten feet behind his take-off.

A mighty gust rattles the windows and flings a rail off the snake fence. The mad November storm pounds relentlessly.

I finish breakfast and listen to the six o'clock news. Our neighbor's yellow patch of broom, bleak in the pewtered light, assures me the sun is above those leaded skies. But the sky is no brighter. A cloud-lined Super Bowl contains our precious bay. Royston has vanished; its homes and skyline lie outside the Bowl. On the other shore, the Spit plays hide-and- seek with the whitecaps. Will we have November light all day?

Surely November hasn't come to stay in June, with summer just three weeks away.

From My Window

School Days

Class of 1932, Listowel High School
Listowel, Ontario

From My Window

DAYLIGHT ON THE HUMBER

The muggy stickiness of Toronto's ninety degree temperature and the ninety percent humidity defies the whirling fan. The air, too heavy to circulate, hangs about my naked body. My watch says four a.m. I never sleep well in a strange bed. Perhaps I can find relief in an early morning walk.

I leave the cool of Humber College's airconditioned lounge, and the air outside feels warmer than my oven-like bedroom. Night still rules the tree-lined streets as sodium lights struggle to push their eerie yellow glare through the mass of leaves.

At an intersection a glimpse skyward reveals the stars but no sign of the new day. Down leaf-tunneled Church Street traffic lights play their musical chairs of red, yellow and green.

At Jane Street, the Flag Shop, its show-windows crammed with flags, makes an United Nations of the corner. A black hulk protrudes on to the sidewalk. I almost trip over the black man huddled on the steps. He could be drunk. Or dead. Or sleeping there to escape the heat. His eyes show white; he's alive and I see the black lunch bucket at his feet. He's waiting for a bus and relaxing as only his race knows how.

Across the street a double-gabled church squats flat and huge like a giant toadstool. A sexy-blue neon sign welcomes me to "The Palace of Prayer, A Multi-Cultural Church", and invites me to "Experience the Difference". In the northeastern sky the hint of dawn shows above the concrete bridge that carries the 401 over Jane Street. Beneath the bridge a spooky yellow-lit tunnel gobbles red taillights and spews out two-eyed monsters as early risers race to work. Above the bridge, and silhouetted against the brightening sky, three tall high-rises stretch towards the fading stars like the bucket teeth on a giant front-end loader. Atop the 401, vehicles flash back and forth like fireflies trailing lights of red.

Fear cringes me as I enter the clammy tunnel. A snorting truck threatens me from the rear; my skin creeps as trucks on 401 rumble over head and shake the concrete walls. I want to run and flee this hell-hole of pounding sound.

The Eastern sky softly floods grassy grounds alongside the 401 and lights the deep, concrete walls of the boxed-in Humber River, revealing the trickle of muddy water on its narrow floor. Litterbugs have scattered what looks like paper across the greenery; now more light shows it's not paper, but the umbrella flowers of wild carrots growing in the untamed grass.

I climb away from the underpass towards a beige coloured building bathed in yellow spotlights sitting atop the hill. What is this jewel doing in this desert of urban despair? THE HEAD OF-FICE OF KENTUCKY FRIED CHICKEN shouts a loud gold-leafed sign. The building sits well back from the exhaust-polluted Jane Street and a large bed of red and white fushias bloom K.F.C. for all the world to see.

The Colonel can't waste this little spot of beauty, so he has built a fancy outlet right next door. He beams from his famous barrel, resting high above Jane Street, and staring at all the potential customers speeding by on 401.

In the block ahead I see the Golden Arches. I could use a cup of coffee. The traffic is growing; a bus full of early shifters rumbles to the city centre. I wait at the corner for the walk sign. There are people in McDonald's and I can almost taste the coffee. One door is locked but another is open. I get one foot inside and a nervous man rushes to the door, "We don't open until six-thirty, sir." He looks worried as if I, with the morning newspaper rolled up under my arm, might hold up the place.

I retrace my steps and, in the brighter light, shadows show the wrinkles of Jane Street's aging. The church, even more toadstool-like, could almost house an elfin family, and the black man has left the Flag Shop.

The sun pinks the eastern sky as I climb the steps to Humber College's Osler Hall. In my stifling bedroom I long for the cool sea breezes caressing our Comox Bay. But it's three thousand miles and three daylight hours away.

COED BATHROOMS

It was my third Elderhostel and I had chosen Toronto's Humber College because I wanted to do more genealogical research of my family history. I'd been accepted for a two-week stay and I liked the six classes they offered. If I got on a hot genealogical trail I could always skip a class or two.

The Elderhostel calender said we'd be staying in single rooms in a nurses' residence, and having seen the quarters my daughter occupied when she was in training, I was prepared for anything. I was surprised at the neat, clean ten-storey brick building pushing skyward through the mantle of maples shading the residental area. It looked better than most Toronto high-rises scattered across the city like awkward giants gawking at the sky.

I had to ring a buzzer to get through the second door of the security entrance. First time I'd encountered locked doors in a college! Were they interested in keeping people in or keeping people out? The air-conditioned rotunda, cafeteria and comfortable lounge were grouped around the entrance, offering pleasant relief from the stifling heat of Toronto's muggy summer.

I registered at the reception desk located across from twin elevators, and got the key to my first-floor room. The single room with a clothes closet had been well cared for — they must train nurses better than college students. A single bed, a sink, desk, three good lights, drawers and filing cabinet made a comfortable and functional room. I'd seen few better; however the good-sized fan couldn't cool the oven-like room. Our floor had a TV room, a laundry, a kitchen with fridge and stove, two pay phones and two phones for incoming calls only. The bathroom had four showers, and four stalls with toilet bowls but no urinals.

After a cafeteria chicken dinner, thirty women and six men

answered the Elderhostel roll call. I felt sorry for hostess Ann Seamans. It was her first experience with Elderhostel. She'd just finished a course in gerontology and would get class credits for being our hostess.

She soon discovered she had some unhappy people. It started with the bus tour. When was the bus tour? "You mean to tell us there's no bus tour! There's supposed to be a bus tour — it says so in the brochure," chorused half a dozen voices.

Poor Anne listened to the complaints, and promised she would try to get a bus tour. I guess it must've been the heat that prompted a lanky irate Yank to get up and walk to the front of the class, waving a threatening finger. He complained about one of the elevators being out of service, no bus trip and no washroom for the men. "If you can't provide better service you shouldn't have these classes. We're on the tenth floor and I have to get up two or three times during the night, and you mean to tell me I have to come down to the second floor every time I need to go to the bathroom?" His angry finger threatened poor Anne's nose.

I'd heard enough. "What the hell do you expect for two hundred Canadian dollars a week? The Waldorf Astoria? If you're so damn unhappy you can have my room on the first floor or you might try peeing in the sink."

I looked around me. What the hell was I doing in this crowd of gray-haired and wrinkled people? If the lanky Yank didn't leave maybe I should.

On the first floor we had no problem with co-educational bathrooms. After all, young people shared the bathrooms. I got used to it. But I must admit that the first time I entered one of the four stalls and saw a woman's slipper under the partition, I locked the door, raised the seat, but changed my mind and sat down to pee. The showers were roomy and partitioned so you had ample room and privacy.

Monday we started classes. Gary Begg, a tall handsome man with a head of prematurely gray hair and sporting the latest in casual summer dress, lectured on "American/Canadian

Relations" --a timely topic with thirty Americans in our group. He knew his subject and his presentation kept most of us awake.

I sat up front and sideways to the class and in the second hour I'd do a sleep count. Most I ever had in Gary's class was four. In the afternoon class one very warm day I counted ten.

Gary did the morning's second hour – a study of Canadian authors. During Gary's lectures the seats never got uncomfortable – a good criteria – as he analyzed the struggle-to-survive theme of Stephen Leacock, Pierre Berton, Farley Mowat, Margaret Laurence, Alice Munro, Jack Hodgins (from Courtenay) and other Canadian writers.

Osler Hall hummed with activity. We gray-haired wonders had to fight for space in the cafeteria with sixty high school kids from Quebec on an English Immersion program. Nurses, students, and out-of-town young people with summer jobs lived on our floor, and got their own meals.

Gary Begg

After classes and in the evenings the building seemed to bulge with bodies. The TV blared, while the reception desk and elevators worked overtime. It all sounded confusing, annoying and some times frightening. There was no escape. It was too hot to stay in your oven-like room, too boisterous in the lounge and much too muggy to sit on the lawn.

By Friday, as I did my sleep count I was amazed to find that my classmates didn't look as old as they had on Sunday. The wrinkles had smoothed. We were enjoying each other's company and joked about the bathrooms.

I remember Leah Lerner best of all. Bright, inquisitive and attractive, she often sparked our discussions by talking beautifully with her hands, like a Hawaiian dancer. Saturday, she was at the desk checking out. "Goodbye, Leah, have a safe trip to Chicago."

"Thank you," she sang, "Oh, I love Toronto. I think it's beautiful. And that Gary Begg, could I go for him. I'd love to live in Toronto but would have to go to Chicago to buy my clothes."

During class Gary read my poem, "New Teeth" and the story, "The Night I Spent in Jail". The class liked them and I got twenty requests for copies of my book. I'm committed now; I'll have to print the book to win.

After a week of Elderhosteling in Humber College's Osler Hall, I was on a first name basis with the staff and most of the young people on the first floor. I helped Norma Thomson, a classmate of Anne Seamens and our hostess for the second week, get started with thirty-eight new oldsters. There were only six Americans in this class; they got their bus tour and I clued them in on co-ed bathrooms.

It had been forty-five years since I lived in a college dorm. In those days there were no shared bathrooms at Regina's Luther College. No way you could get past Miss Walters into the girls residence; and Mr. Stouffer, the men's dean, was even tougher.

None of us had cars. Occasionally we got Dad's car, but we also got a sister or baby brother to take along. Then came those long, wide American cars and lots of quiet side roads and safe lovers' lanes in which to park. Later still, came the furnished van with stereo and rock.

But times have changed. Now there are "Osler Halls" with co-ed bathrooms, fridges to cool your beer, electric stoves and microwaves, washing machines and dryers. You sign your friend in and sign out by 11 p.m. Sure beats a cold prairie car, or even a rock and roll van.

Shaw said, "The bedroom combines the maximum of temptation with the maximum of opportunity." As I watched the flow of vibrant humanity pass the reception desk, and saw the goings and comings on the twin elevators, I remembered Luther College, our old Model A Ford and Dad's fancy Moon, and wondered what I was doing on the first floor of Osler Hall secretly envying the vitality of youth.

Margy

Margy, tall, slim and good-looking with her ready smile, roomed across the hall from the lounge by the pay phones. You could always tell when she was home. She never closed her door, and a cluster of people blocked the hallway. She spent hours on the phone and seemed to mother-hen the whole floor.

Amick, a Quebec girl in the English Immersion program, was attracted to my laptop computer, read "The Night I Spent in Jail" to test her English, and asked for a copy of my book.

Greg, my next door neighbor was a monitor; he enforced the

133

curfew and made single occupancy compulsory. I never found out how he did it, but he had great repartee with the Quebecers.

Marcel, the self-appointed leader of the French Canadians, husky, blonde and a woman-charmer, liked my Nike basketball sneakers. While we watched the Montreal and Edmonton teams play football, I bet on Edmonton when they were ten points down and won the bet. He didn't have the two bucks, but I won a friend!

Pierre, round and tubby, watched cartoons, loved to talk and try out his new language on anyone who'd listen. He ate constantly, stuffing himself with chocolate bars, potato chips and pop from the cafeteria's vending machines.

And there was Donna. I almost tripped over her low-swung wheelchair as it rounded the corner and raced past me, then swung to a halt at the lounge door. I watched the blonde bomber as she grabbed the heavy fire-door, braced one arm against the jam, yanked the door open and bulled her wheel-chair through.

Margaret Roser, a New Orleans' Elderhosteler and a first - floorer was also on her second week. "I'm used to the heat," she said, "New Orleans is muggy most of the time, but I find the bedrooms here unbearable."

"Have you got used to the co-educational bathrooms?"

"Oh yes! But one day I saw bare feet and a hairy gorilla leg under the partition. I almost screamed. I wanted to run, but I didn't. I locked the door and waited until my woolly companion left. I can't stand hairy men."

"I'm enjoying my association with the young people on our floor. How about you?"

"I'm glad they're not my kids — but I wouldn't mind being one of them. They enjoy life more than I ever did. They've made me feel younger and better than I've felt for years. I think its helped my arthritis — yesterday I forgot to use my cane! This is my first Elderhostel, and I'd like to come back to Osler Hall."

So would I.

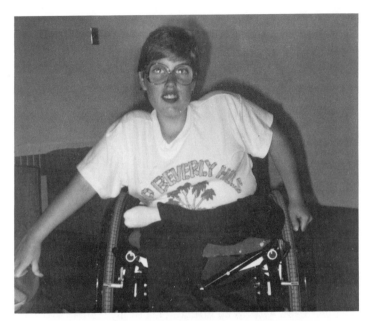

DONNA OF HUMBER'S OSLER HALL

I feel uncomfortable with people in wheel-chairs and their obvious disabilities. But Donna wore a sweet smile and seemed right at home on our boisterous first floor. I admired her spunk and wondered how she kept so ordinary. I tried to help her open the heavy door, but she ignored me completely, and with astonishing ease sailed through and dashed down the hall.

She fitted snugly into her wheel-chair, her rag-doll legs tucked close against an almost square body, topped with a fine-featured face, peach complexion, bright blue bright eyes and a tousle of soft blonde hair. She looked blocky as if she had grown up inside a half-pint milk carton. She had trouble eating at the cafeteria tables and used the coffee table in the lounge. She scooted along the halls, opening the heavy fire-doors and beaming independence in every move.

She fascinated me. I wanted to know more about this whirlwind in a box. I found her alone in the lounge. "I've been wanting to talk to you. Would you mind doing an interview?"

"I don't see why not. You seem like a pretty decent guy," she replied.

"I'll get the key to the classroom and my tape recorder and we'll try it now. Okay?"

"That'll be fine."

"The air-conditioning works well in this room. Are you comfortable? This is my first attempt at interviewing anyone, and I hope I don't embarrass you or ask any awkward questions. If I do, please tell me."

"Don't worry, I will."

"I've watched you and admired you. Tell me about your disability."

"I was born with spina bifida. Part of my spinal cord was exposed. They operated within three hours and patched it up as best they could, but it left me without the use of my legs."

She tucked her rag-doll legs tightly against her body, looking legless and cube-like. "In spina bifida excess water often collects in the brain causing enlargement of the skull. To drain the excess fluid a 'shunt' is installed. It's a tube going from the brain to the stomach. Mine doesn't function any more because my condition has stabilized.

"Spina bifida ranges from 'almost normal' to people who die in early infancy. A friend and I flew to England on an exchange program and the pressure change of the flight affected the functioning of her shunt. She died a week after we got home."

"Was she badly disabled?"

"No, she wasn't. She was about my age, we'd had a great time in England. I miss her".

"I'm sorry. Sometimes life's not fair."

She smiled as a tear smudged her eye.

136

"You have a lovely smile and I like the way you use it."

"Thank you."

"May I take your picture? I'll do a portrait, and may I take one showing your disability?"

"I don't often let people take my picture, and I hate it when people stare at me."

"Are you envious of other people?"

"Not really. I've lived all my life without the use of my legs, so to me that's normal. I've adapted to my handicap and I seldom think about it, but I'd like to have a few things that money can buy. I'd love to have my own van. I told my Dad that's what I want for my twenty-first birthday."

"Have you had unpleasant experiences in public?"

"Not often. But one day I was waiting for our bus and three tough kids gave me a bad time. Called me horrible names and belittled my legs and the shape of my body. They eventually got tired and left.

"Then a woman came from across the street; said she'd pray for me. Asked me if I'd been saved, and said if I accepted Jesus as my Saviour I'd get well. She wouldn't leave me alone. She said I was suffering from the sins of my parents, and if I didn't ask Jesus into my life I'd burn in hell. Finally our bus rescued me. She was gross."

"Are you ever bitter that you've been denied the use of your legs?"

"I'm not bitter but at times I get lonely. When I was eight I had a lot of surgery and it was painful. I learned to suffer alone and now I enjoy being alone. I don't dislike people but I'm more comfortable with me."

"Have you any brothers or sisters?"

"Two sisters and a brother."

"Are they okay?"

"Yes, but I hardly know them. When I was three and a half I

went to the Rumsey Medical Centre and I've lived there most of my life. I had to learn to do things for myself and give not only 110 percent but 120 percent. I'm independent, and I'll never accept anything I haven't earned. I go where the hell I like, and if I get fed up, I go out and get drunk."

"Ever get picked up for impaired driving in your wheelchair?"

"No, but people with motorized wheel-chairs have."

"Do you have one?"

"No, I can go twice as fast in this wheel-chair. They're just poop-pots as far as I'm concerned."

"I know children can be cruel. Are they cruel to *you?*"

"I've never lived with normal children, but the ones I meet are curious and they want to know why I don't have regular legs, and they like my wheel-chair. It's the parents who are cruel. They warn their kids not get too close or touch me, as if I had AIDS, or something."

"Are you religious?"

"I believe in God. I'm a Christian. But I'm not worried about what's going to happen to me when I die. I've got all I can do to live this life. I know I won't live as long as most people so to me every moment is precious. I want to enjoy life here and now and live it to the full."

Her philosophy amazed me. "Have you ever read Keyes' *Handbook to Higher Consciousness*? He was a quadriplegic and writes about living in the here-and-now, and about not putting conditions on your love."

"I believe that. Give your love unconditionally. Give it for the joy of loving, not for the love it might bring. I have to deal with my own condition. I can probably accept people easier than you can."

"Have you ever been in love?"

"Yes, I've been in love. Just because my legs don't work, and I've got a hump on my back, doesn't mean I'm different! I'm not in love right now. I hope some day I'll marry and share my life and love."

"What kind of dreams do you have?"

"I'm never in a wheel-chair in my dreams."

"Do you have two good legs?"

"Oh yes! Until I was ten years old I believed that some morning I'd wake up and be able to walk. I used to swing my legs over the edge of the bed and try to stand up. I'd fall flat on my face and often hurt myself.

"In my dreams my legs are long and slim. I walk with grace, I bound up stairs and I dance on air. It's wonderful.

"But in the end my feet begin to drag, I feel something horrible trying to catch me and I wake up screaming. My dreams don't always end up in nightmares. When I'm dancing with my strong arms wrapped around my Prince Charming, I awake hugging my teddy bear or my pillow. I always remember the dance."

"The dance?"

"I love to go to dances. I watch every move the dancers make and I listen to every word in the songs. I love it! I love it! *I love it* "

"You must have lots of rhythm in your soul. Do you play a musical instrument?"

"I used to play the clarinet, but I don't now."

"Why?"

"It bothered my shunt and gave me awful headaches. I had a hangover every time I practiced."

"Do you play any sports?"

"Sure. I like rugby best of all. We play it with a soft sponge ball. It's kind of rough and tumble but I don't mind the knocks. I can hold my own. We play volley ball and I've tried tennis but it's too tough to hit the ball."

"What's your favorite TV sport?"

"Basketball, and the Celtics are my team. I just worship 'The

Bird'. I root for the Blue Jays and cheer for the Maple Leafs and the Argos. Sometimes they take a bus load of us to a football game and we get to sit right down of the field. It's neat."

"I've enjoyed talking to you, Donna, and I feel I'm a better person for knowing you. I'll keep in touch and put you on my Christmas mailing list. I write a family letter each year, I think you'll like it. One more question: how should I or anybody else approach a disabled person?"

"The same as you'd approach anybody else. Just remember we are real, whole living people. We don't want to be reminded of our disability and most of all we don't want pity. I still have great plans for my life, though not half as many as I had when I was younger — I know my limitations now. I must be realistic and not envy other people's money, cars and legs.

"You just be yourself; the guys and gals on our first floor think you're kinda special. It's been fun talking to you, Gordon. I've put you on my 'Love List'."

THE BOSS'S DESK

He'd been awake for hours. Shadows of the leafless maple tree flickered against the misty window. The gloomy gleam of the street light vaguely lit the room. Jonathan Hargraves waited for dawn to erase the spooky shadows. He watched as the room grayed, revealing the outline of his gilt-framed portrait at the foot of the bed. He hoped a burst of yellow might brighten the new day. He always looked better in the sunlight.

"My, I was a handsome and distinguished man," he said to himself. "Those were great days!"

He couldn't remember when he hadn't been good-looking. His mother and grandmother had doted on him when he was a small boy, dressing him in fluffy blouses and velvet pants.

When he started school they insisted he be meticulously groomed. He hated it at first and got roughed up a couple of times, but he soon discovered the teachers liked and encouraged his tidiness and gentle behavior. He never found his lessons difficult and breezed through all his classes.

He'd been in high school when the dirty thirties hit. In the middle of his last year, his father died. The family had to accept relief, and Jonathan quit school. He walked the city streets for days, scanned the help-wanted ads, called back day after day in his hopeless search.

On the morning of his nineteenth birthday he'd decided he'd buy a new outfit. Tip Top Tailors had suits for nineteen dollars. He'd take the plunge. You had to be well-dressed to succeed. Tip-Top suits were made-to-measure.

"I need a new outfit," he told Tip Top's eager clerk.

"Yes sir, we have it gutt choice from fabrics. Samples are new, yesterday from Toronto coming. A three-piece suit, double breasted, I am giving you for nineteen dollars. And for my first customer today, I give it for the same price a shirt and a very nice tie. Come Mister, have it once a look."

"Mr. Hargraves, — Jonathan C. Hargraves. I'm new in town. I've accepted a position with Sheaffer Pen. I start to work a week from today. Could you have a suit ready?"

"Mr. Hargraves you come it back one week. Suit she's ready. You pay it cash or maybe you use it easy-pay plan, two dollars now down und two dollars a week?"

"I usually pay cash. But I'll take advantage of your payment plan."

He'd never forget the day he walked out of Tip Top's store in his made-to-order suit. A halo of well-dressed confidence followed him down Main Street, to the 7th floor of the Scott Building and the main office of Sheaffer Pen.

He'd scouted the company office. Mr. R.B. Boswell was president and sales manager. "Is Mr. Boswell in?" he asked.

"Is he expecting you?" said the receptionist.

"Tell him J.C. Hargraves, Parker Pen's leading salesman, would like to see him."

R.B. Boswell was sitting behind the same desk shown in the portrait. He soon discovered the brazen young man knew nothing about selling pens. But Jonathan did sell himself and he joined the sales staff of Sheaffer Pen, and vowed that one day he'd sit behind Boswell's desk.

It had taken twenty years. He remembered his trips to his tailor, being measured, selecting the tie and shirt and the cream-coloured vest, and the final fitting at Main Street's exclusive haberdashery.

Now as the morning light brightened his portrait, he could see the colours and well-groomed lines of his clothes. The photographer had captured his stern importance, his neatly groomed hair and his crisp mustache. He admired the arrangement of the Sheaffer pens, the desk clock and his copy of the *Financial Post* tucked to one side.

He heard the morning footsteps and the click of the light switch. As his hospital room brightened to the soft fluorescent light, he rolled his eyes to see who his orderly was this morning. He hated the damn mornings, hated being changed and cleaned like a baby, hated being asked the same stupid questions every morning and answering "yes" with one blink of his eyes and "no" with two blinks.

When he was fed, bathed, and bedded in clean sheets, his portrait took on new life in the better light, and he wondered about his new clothes. He had worn them only once — his first day at the boss's desk.

VERBS

Verbs are to writers what diamonds are to girls — their best friend. I love 'em.

The word "verb" is a noun, says Webster's Unabridged Dictionary and means "any of a class of words expressing action, existence or occurrence." Verbs are the work horses of language. Active verbs make people live. Without verbs, the nouns-- bricks coloured and shaped by adjectives and adverbs -- would never leave the brick yard. These verbal workers of language build our wordy castles, hold the parts together and store our thoughts in the halls of knowledge.

Verbs perform wonders. A verb can take you into the past faster than a time machine. Add "ed" or change a "d" to "t" and speed back a thousand years. Add "will", and without returning home, whisk yourself into the future and view tomorrow from the spaceship of your mind.

Verbs are rich. Roget's Thesaurus give us fifty ways to walk. Your character may step, stride or saunter. If he's in a hurry, he may run, race or speed.

The power of verbs convolutes the brain, warms the skin or chills the heart. Verbs stir our emotions when we jump with fear or blush with shame; send hormones of love cruising the blood stream to make a heart-beat race; alert the eyes to the exquisite softness of a beautiful woman; thrill to the touch of silken skin, and the furriness of fresh-washed hair; scent the perfume of a rose or smell the rat lurking in the strange dark.

Verbs used in metaphors transform people into animals and animals into people. D.H. Lawrence's Bertie becomes a broken-shelled mollusc. William Faulkner has Sarty's stomach read the labels on the cans. Stephan Crane has the sun swing like a pendulum in the sky.

Verbs roam the recesses of my mind. I'll find the words I need, and sharply hone selections to describe the senses I feel. They will enrich my five senses to help me find the elusive sixth. Verbs will help me create stories for my imagined readers.

AIRLINE PICKPOCKET

Hello, Operator, I want to call New York 216-339-2662 and reverse the charges. My name is Max Silverman.

"It's a pay phone, Operator. Uh uh, lemme see — Yah! It's 714-497-1524.

"Yes, Operator.

"That's okay, Operator, I'll be glad to call A.T.& T. again.

"Hello, Mama. This is Sonny.

"Yes, Mama, it's your Sonny. No Mama — I'm in the Los Angeles Airport.

"Yes, yes, Mama, everything is fine. Is Papa home?

"Oh! I see. Well — I had a little accident, Mama.

"No. Nothing serious, Mama. Well I met this girl —

"Yes, Mama, a Gentile girl —

144

"No, Mama, I didn't fall in love with a Gentile girl again —

"Just let me explain, Mama. Please, Mama —

"No, Mama, I didn't lose my cherry. I lost my wallet. I'm broke, Mama.

"No, I can't call Uncle Sammy. I don't have a quarter.

"Yes, Mama, I know a good Jewish girl would never steal your wallet. But Mama, I have to have some money!

"I know it's just an hour to the Sabbath. But —

"I *am* thinking of Papa's heart —

Mama, will you please phone Uncle Sammy and tell him I'm at the airport? Ask him to call me. I'll wait by this pay phone. The number's 714-497-1524. Listen Mama —

"I know Papa doesn't like your brother, but Mama, I'm broke and Uncle Sammy's my only hope. Papa could wire some money to him.

"Mama, I've tried to find the girl.

"Yes, Mama dear, I've told the police. Mama, will you please listen —

"I can't help that now, Mama. Won't you please phone Uncle Sammy before the Sabbath starts? You know your brother never moves once the sun sets.

"Yes, Mama, I've learned my lesson. I thought she was a nice girl. Just call Uncle Sammy. Please Mama.

"Mama, if you can't get Uncle Sammy, call me back.

"Thanks, Mama. I'll wait, Mama. Goodbye, Mama."

I hang up and there are three people waiting to use the pay phone. I go to the end of the line. The first two calls are short, but the third caller is a teen-ager and he's having an argument with his girl friend. Will he ever hang up? Finally he bangs the receiver on the hook and mumbles, "To hell with her!"

I start to explain my trouble to the lady behind me when the phone rings. "Cripes! Hope that's Uncle Sammy," I say as I grab the warm receiver.

"Hello?

"Yes, this is Sonny Silverman. Is that you Uncle Sammy?

"Gosh! Am I ever glad to hear your voice.

"I'll be right right outside the Pan-Am terminal. Right by the loading area.

"No, that's fine, Uncle Sammy. We can go right to the synagogue.

"Yes, Uncle Sammy, I'll watch out for those Gentile girls.

"Thank you. I'll be watchin' for you. Goodbye Uncle Sammy."

146

Modern Times

The Editor and the Author

From My Window

ROY'S REPAIR

We travel together, Cleo and I. She's a '77 blue Mercedes and we've been going together for 150,000 miles. She's a joy to drive and we look forward to the six hundred mile, two-day trip from Calgary to Vancouver. The clear October night has cocooned her in a thin blanket of white, but at the first turn of the switch she springs to life and quietly purrs while I scrape the frost from her windshield and windows. Her clock says five a.m.

I snuggle into her wool-covered contoured seat, feed her well at the first all-night service station, guide her through Calgary's deserted streets and head west on the Trans-Canada Highway. I set the cruise control at the speed limit plus 10. A dim announcement of the new day erases the stars behind us.

149

Ahead a full moon silhouettes the jagged peaks of the Rockies. Dawn shrouds the foothills. The mountains creep towards us, their evergreen skirts decorated with clusters of yellow aspens and red patches of vine maples. Their peaks glisten with a fresh dusting of snow. Between the tree line and the hem of the snow, naked rock adds soft tones of purple, gray and brown.

We pass Banff and corkscrew through the mountains. Cleo loves the well-engineered super-elevated curves of the winding road. She reacts like a thoroughbred. I hold her in check as a sign warns of curves ahead. We ease into the turn then I give her her head. She hugs the road, responding to the throttle, to the wheel and the stick. We pull up behind a crawling camper. She champs at the bit as I patiently wait for an opening. She senses the passing lane and I give her free rein. She leaps ahead and charges into the next curve.

We stop for refreshments; I take coffee, Cleo gulps a tank of gas. Rested, we swing back to the highway and accelerate into the next curve. She responds sluggishly. "What's the matter, Cleo? Are you feeling tired already? You don't suppose they gave you the wrong kinda gas back there?"

It's downhill for the next couple of miles, but I can tell — Cleo's sick. The road levels as it follows a creek. I shift down to third, and rev the motor but Cleo refuses to go more than thirty. We pull over. I check the panel, the engine, underneath, inside and outside and kick the wheels for good luck. We try again. But thirty is the limit.

We're ten miles from Golden, five horizontal miles and two thousand vertical feet from the continental divide and the summit of the Rocky Mountains.

"Dammit, Cleo! We gotta get to the top of that bloody mountain. You don't want to be towed into Golden, do you? If you can chug us to the top, it'll be all down-hill into Golden."

With hazard lights flashing, an embarrassed Mercedes and a red-faced driver coax 'the world's best engineered car' along the graveled shoulder. We finally top the last crest, coast for five miles and stagger into Golden's first service station.

We're in luck. A sign says "Mechanic on Duty". Cleo dies at the pump. I arouse a dozing attendant.

"Is your mechanic around?" I inquire.

"He doesn't work Mondays. It's his day off."

I describe Cleo's ailments to him and ask if he can tell me where I might get some help.

"Try Roy's Repair. Roy loves Mercedes's." He draws me a map.

"Come on, Cleo. Let's find Roy. I know you're hurting, but it can't be far." We stagger over Golden's graveled roads. I spot "Roy's Repair" and pull up in the lane.

The corrugated iron building rusts in a graveyard of crippled cars. I pick my way around the wrecks and step through an undersize door into the garage.

The garage smell of oil, gas and tobacco smoke strikes first. The place is crowded, almost packed. A Ford van suffering from a ruptured radiator sits over one hoist; over the other a headless pickup gets a valve job. A tool bench runs along the back wall. A red well-gauged testing apparatus fights for space. Against the far wall a pot-bellied stove battles to warm the oily air. Tucked behind the stove on an old bus seat, an old man nurses a cup of coffee. A two-by-four wash room squeezes in the corner, a green grease-stained door tries to hide the battered sink and toilet bowl. Against the washroom wall, a waist-high desk holds loads of scattered papers, books and junk mail. A teen-aged girl stuffed into bib overalls works on the Ford van. A teen-aged boy with black oil up to his elbows threatens to disappear into the bowels of the pickup. At the work bench a middle-aged man, wearing a black skull cap and once-white coveralls dismantles a carburetor. Nobody notices me. I ask Skullcap, "Are you Roy?"

"No. Roy's next door in the radiator shop."

I find Roy. He's busy soldering a radiator and at the same time talking to a woman about Golden's civic problems. They pay no attention to me. Roy is tall and gaunt with wisps of thin red hair following the nods of his head. A pair of baggy pants hangs dangerously from his narrow hips, and a green greased-smudged sweat shirt falls three inches short of his belt, revealing his slightly-potted belly. I wait patiently, admiring the skill of his long fingers as they heal the damaged radiator. Finally I interrupt. "Are you Roy?"

"Yup! What can I do for you?" he asks.

I describe Cleo's symptoms. "I'll take a look at her as soon as I finish here. Sure hope she doesn't need parts. Takes four days to get anything from Calgary and just as long to come from Vancouver."

I picture myself land-locked in Golden for four or five days. Five days in a motel in Golden? Good God ...

Alternatives flash through my mind. I could fly out. Maybe hitch a ride to Vancouver. I have to be there by noon on Wednesday.

He finishes the soldering, extinguishes the torch, and the woman and I follow him out of the shop. "Bring her around to the front," he commands. Cleo complains, but manages to drag herself to the front of the shop. The big door rolls up.

Roy wastes no time, "Open her up," he demands. I raise the hood revealing Cleo's private parts to this brash, strange man.

"Here's part of your problem," he points to a broken hose. "Who services your car?"

"Three Point Motors in Victoria."

"I'll have to phone them. Have to charge you for the phone call."

"That's okay. Here's their phone number — and the shop foreman's name is Wagner." He disappears for a few minutes and returns with some tools. He clamps a tube, and reconnects a rubber hose.

"Try that," he says.

Cleo seems to respond better but refuses to climb the incline to the highway, so I nurse her back to the garage.

"Must be the converter. The damn things are a bloody nuisance. I'll have to phone Victoria again," he grumbles.

I watch him phone. He hangs up and lolls over to where I'm waiting for the bad news.

"The converter should be opened and cleaned out. Trouble is nobody here can weld aluminum, so that's out. Could disconnect the exhaust in front of the converter, but that'd drive you deaf and crazy before you'd get to Vancouver. If you drive that car any further the way she is now, you'll ruin the valves. New converter could cost you four hundred bucks and probably take a week to get here. Let's put her up on the hoist and see what we can do." He rolls up the garage door and I follow him.

"Gotta get that damn Ford outa here," he grumbles. "How the hell's that radiator coming, Mary?" he asks as he pushes her aside, grabs a creeper and with six inches of his bare belly exposed, slides under the van. He hollers for tools, grunts and swears and emerges spotted with a new covering of grease and mud. He connects a couple of hoses, tells Mary to give the Ford a drink, starts the van and backs it out of the garage. He's rough and ready ... and efficient.

"Drive her onto the hoist," he orders. With Cleo high in the air Roy attacks her under-belly. He drills two one inch holes in the base of the converter about three inches apart. With nose pliers he pulls and tugs to remove a tough wire mesh guarding the honeycombed innards of the converter. He rips the converter's guts apart with a pneumatic chisel. Mary and the boy fight with long-nosed pliers to open a passageway through the blocked converter.

Suddenly Roy announces, "It's lunch time. We shut 'er right down or we'd never get anything to eat. Better come with us. There's a small cafe down the street. Makes fine soup."

He locks and bars all the doors and leads me to the longest station wagon I have ever seen, "Hop in," he says.

I get in. There's no seat on the driver's side, nothing but a squashed cardboard box. He swings himself in, his long legs parallel to the floor. He grasps the steering wheel and pulls himself up to peer through the spokes. Only his head is higher than the door. Ichabod Crane rides again, I think, but don't say so.

The small cafe becomes the Shell Restaurant on the Trans-Canada. Roy leads us to a booth. He's greeted on all sides.

"Hi, Roy."

"How ya doin', Roy?"

"What's new, Roy?"

He nods his replies.

"Would you like a menu?"

"No. Just bring me the best steak sandwich you have, medium rare, and a side order of chips."

"Make it two," I say.

During the meal, I learn he's a Social Creditor, but he's not happy with Premier Bennett. "No guts, not half the man his father was. W.A.C. Bennett was the best Premier the damn province ever had. Anyway, we're too damn far from Victoria. We should be part of Alberta. Calgary's a hell of a lot closer, and cheaper, too."

I pick up the bill, happy to keep our man in sight. Never know when Ichabod Crane might decide to take the afternoon off.

Back at the garage, Roy inspects the gutted converter. "That's okay," he tells his kids. "The exhaust will blow through there now."

He's taken a five inch bar of iron, drilled and threaded holes in both ends. Now he works the bar through the holes in the converter, gets the holes in the end of the bar directly over the holes in the converter, takes wide-headed bolts with wider washers, and screws then into the bar. The holes are tightly sealed. It's an ingenious device!

"Take her for a spin," he says, "and give her hell."

I know at once Cleo's feeling better. We ease into the highway traffic and head up the hill that four hours earlier we'd

limped down. Cleo scampers up like a frisky filly. We wheel back
to Roy's Repair. In front of the garage Cleo purrs gratefully, a
smile on her grill.

"She runs like a dream, Roy. Better than ever! Give me your
bill and I'll be on my way."

"I'll have to charge you for those phone calls. Have to phone
the operator." He searches his desk for his invoices, finds them
and I watch him prepare my bill. He hands me the hand-written
account. It says $61.50, for Pete's sake! You don't get inside the
door at Three Point Motors for less than a hundred.

I hand him eighty dollars, saying, "Keep the change." And he
thanks me!

"By the way, Roy, what's your last name?"

"Same as that son of a bitch that was president of the United
States."

"Nixon?"

"That's right," he grins.

I shake his callused grease-lined hand. "Well, you're a genius, you know. I'm damn glad I found you. You're a great guy — and an A-1 mechanic. I'll stop by the next time I go through Golden."

I guide a fully-recovered Cleo back onto the Trans-Canada, obeying the 30 mph limit. We pass the Shell Restaurant, happily bombing down the highway. A wreath of blue arcs over the Cascades — we're heading for sunshine. Cleo spots the maximum-speed sign. I feel her tug my foot. I bridle her with the cruise control as she sprints into the straight-away and sees the curve ahead.

"Cleo baby, you haven't run so well for ages. Lets go, kiddo!"

"Hold it, Vancouver, here we come!"

AIRPORT MONSTER

Ivy had planned to fly home, to be there when our granddaughter played a leading role in *Fiddler on The Roof* at Comox High, but she'd changed her mind. So her Western Airlines ticket — from Phoenix to Comox, via Vancouver — also had to be changed.

She had flown south on an excursion fare the airline uses to entice Canadian "Snowbirds" to winter in Arizona's sunshine. Her ticket was good only for Western's Flight 403 on the 11th of March. Now she'd be flying home on the 13th of April.

We've gone through all this before. You can't do the change by phone; you have to go to the ticket counter at the airport. You cancel your excursion fare, they issue you a new ticket (a regular one-way fare) and you pay the difference — in American funds, of course — a painful $1.42 for each U.S. dollar.

Since I was going near the Phoenix airport I'd exchange it today. But the traffic thickened as I neared the airport, and I suddenly remembered. *My gosh, it's Friday! Oh well, I'm this close, I'll give it a try ...*

The parking meter ticket said 10:58 a.m. I'd have half an hour for a dollar. It didn't take that long the last time ...

Inside the terminal the weekend's ant-like scramble swarmed around the baggage carousel. The double escalators tumbled people onto the arrival floor. Line-ups plugged the U-drive and ticket counters. Kids and students jabbered everywhere. *My God! I've hit the beginning of the spring break!* American West had four lines jammed against their ticket counter, and the place buzzed with the glee of happy, class-free students. I'd sure picked the wrong day to change Ivy's ticket!

Western's counter was almost deserted. I chose one of the vacant wickets. The short, navy blue-uniformed clerk wore Western's logo and a name tag saying she was Shirley. "Can I help you, sir?" she smiled.

I explained the problem and handed her the ticket. I'm never able to decipher airline tickets. I just hand them over and hope the portion that will take me home is still attached.

"We've booked a reservation for the 13th of April on our morning flight to Vancouver, and continuing to Comox on Air BC."

Her well-manicured fingernails danced across the keyboard, while her brown-specked eyes ping-ponged the computer's monitor. She paused, checked the ticket and reread the screen. "Ummm ..." she muttered.

Again her fingers talked to the computer. Her eyes widened, and the first trace of a frown tilted her eye brows, and the cowlick in her neat up-swept Clairol-blonde hair twitched.

She attacked the little green-eyed monster a third time. Then, exasperated, she placed her hands on the counter, arm-lengthened herself from the stubborn machine, and breathed a quiet "Damn!"

Her eyes scanned the counter for help, "Mary, can you come here for a minute?"

Mary, a tall, straight-haired blonde towered over Shirley's shoulder. She brushed back her bangs, and her cold, onyx-black eyes attacked the flashing screen, as she listened to Shirley's problem. "Try code 767," she said.

Now two pairs of eyes followed the bouncing ball, and Shirley's chattering keyboard tackled Ivy's plan to fly from Phoenix to Comox.

I'm afraid of airport computers — they always win. But I bravely asked, "What's the trouble?"

"On April 1st, Western is being taken over by Delta, and this is the first time we've had to change a fare. Nobody thought to tell the computer," said Shirley.

The computer refused to budge. I could almost hear its cries of indignation.

A man in a navy-blue business suit with a long-service Delta Airlines' pin in the lapel, patrolled behind the counter. "Mr. Mack, can you help us?" asked Mary.

He squeezed his vested, stylish paunch between the two women, and as he listened to their problem his stubby finger raced across the keyboard. He paused, read the screen, shook his head, mumbled, and tried again.

It took him three tries before he smiled, and Shirley and Mary beamed. "There it is. It's a difference of $76 — but that's in Canadian dollars. There's no use fooling around with the computer. Take it into my office and straighten it out."

"I'll be back," said Shirley, gathering the tickets and disappearing into a door at the far end of the counter. I stood by the vacant wicket and waited.

Western's wickets got busier. People started to line up behind me, and I directed them to another line. Fifteen minutes later Shirley returned. "I've booked Mrs. Wagner on Delta's morning flight to Vancouver, but it leaves at 9:45 a.m. instead of 9:15. Will that be okay?"

"Yes, as long as she can get her flight to Comox."

"I'll be right back," she said and once more disappeared into the bowels of the airport.

I waited. And I waited. I stood on one foot, then the other. Even tried two for a change. People continued to line up behind me and I continued to steer them to the longer lines. Some thanked me; others glared at me in disgust before moving to another line. I finally retreated to a seat where I could see the wicket.

Fifteen minutes passed — I'd been there over an hour. I asked the man with the long-service Delta-pin, "Can I leave the tickets with you and pick up the new ones another day?"

"No. You have to pay for them now, or make the reservation again." I returned to my observation post ... and waited.

Western must have booked a plane load while I sat there, because the crowds had deserted their wickets. But the place still hummed with excited travelers.

When I checked the wicket again, they'd changed shifts. A new set of faces sat behind the little green monsters. Maybe Shirley had left ... I'd lost my observation seat, so once more I leaned against the counter.

I saw the blonde cowlick bobbing toward the wicket. Her face was flushed, and her eyes on the verge of tears. "I'm terribly sorry, but I've had a horrible time. Your wife's flight from Vancouver to Comox was on Canadian Pacific, and they're now Pacific Western. Mrs. Wagner's ticket showed a $29 fare from Vancouver to Comox, and nobody ever heard of a $29 fare. So now the difference is $146, and that's American, so I'll need $207 Canadian." she sighed. "I almost forgot, there's a $10 penalty. Isn't that awful? Do you think you'll ever fly Delta again?"

"It's not Delta, it's the little green devil hiding behind the screen in your computer..."

The noon-high sun had curled the parking ticket I'd left on my dash. I straightened it and checked my watch. It said 1:05. I'd been parked for over two hours!

It cost me another five dollars before the attendant would raise the red striped bar and let my Toyota and I escape from the parking lot.

I sighed in relief as the spunky little car dug into the blacktop, and fled out onto the freeway — away from the airport's green-eyed monster. I checked our speed ... Oh my God! An orange-lit screen spread across my dash.

Even my damn car was computerized!

THE GIRL I FORGOT TO SAVE

Wardair's flight 301 was scheduled to leave Toronto for Vancouver at nine a.m. I had seat 25K, a window seat on the right-hand side, helpful for my better ear.

By ten to nine the boarding area at Gate 20 was empty. I'd lingered over a farewell coffee with my niece Olga and her son, so I was the last passenger on board.

A sea of faces stared as I struggled to indian-file my briefcase, my laptop computer and my arm-draped raincoat down the DC 9's skinny aisle.

I spotted my empty seat and the attractive head of amber-blonde hair occupying the adjacent one. Fine ... I'd have female company to Vancouver.

"Excuse me," I said as I stored my things overhead. The smartly-tailored woman stood, and I slipped into 25K. I buckled up, stealing tactful glances and speculating on her age and her occupation. The stylish beige suit blended with her shoulder length hair. Slim, tall and a bit mannish, she could be a business executive. Yet the slightly wrinkled, not-too-new suit suggested an academic. Turning the pages of a paperback about Canadian geography, her long fingers with well-manicured natural nails implied brains. A 35 mm camera and slim leather briefcase tucked under the seat in front of her hinted at research. A single, heavy, yet modest band of gold ringed her wedding finger. No diamonds. She had class, poise and self assurance — and she'd probably read all the way to Vancouver.

I checked the *Globe and Mail* headlines and the sport page. We're typical Canadians, I thought. Won't say a word to one another during the whole flight.

I studied her face. Smooth soft skin showed a trace of wrinkles, yet glowed youthfully through just a hint of skillfully applied make-up. Each time she turned a page she brushed back the veil of silky hair hiding her profile, revealing a finely chiseled nose. I tried not to stare at the neo-Grecian profile as she concentrated on the geology of Yellowknife.

Wardair broke the ice. They served a breakfast salad – a small plate of weathered orange, grapefruit and melon slices with half a limp strawberry thrown in for colour. "I don't often get a fruit salad for breakfast," I remarked. "How's yours?"

"Not too bad," she replied, and I detected an accent.

"Doing some research in the North?" I gestured at her book. "Planning a trip to Yellowknife?"

"No. I picked this up in the gift shop."

"Do you live in Vancouver?"

"No. Toronto." She turned to face me, extended her hand. "I'm Theresa Griffin."

"I'm Gordon Wagner. I live on Vancouver Island. Just spent a week doing research on my family history in the Kitchener-Waterloo area. I'm trying to write a story about my ancestors."

"I've always wanted to do that. I write reports and papers on projects, and I just finished taking an introductory computer course. I want to learn to use a word processing program."

"I've been using a computer for a couple of years. It's a great way to write. Which program are you learning?"

"I've started on WordPerfect, but I don't really know how to use it."

"I use WordPerfect all the time. I have a laptop computer in the overhead compartment. After breakfast I'll get it down and show you how my Toshiba 1100 + handles WordPerfect."

I learned she was on her way to visit her son and daughter who live with her first husband. With a Master's degree in Developmental Psychology, she had taught in the slums of Philadelphia and worked for the city's Welfare Department while her husband got his doctorate in Town Planning. She had grown up in Newfoundland, which explained the accent, and she had strong opinions on the seal hunt. She had a wealth of stories to tell.

I told her about Gabriele Rico's *Writing the Natural Way*, and how I used it to enter my right mind and retrieve my subconscious memories. We played with my laptop computer; I showed her what it would do and demonstrated how the Speller and the Thesaurus worked. She read a couple of the stories I had on my data disk, and liked them.

"I'd like to have a copy of your book. And I think you should send some of these stories to Peter Gzowsky of the CBC."

"If you give me your address I'll be glad to send you one."

"I don't have a card with me. I'll write it on this --"

"Why don't you just print it on the computer and I'll enter it in my address book when I get home?"

She did -- typed it neatly and clearly on my computer's screen.

The trip to Vancouver was one of the shortest I'd ever flown. She said the same. Her son was seventeen and her daughter fourteen and she was anxious to spend as much time as possible with them, so she was one of the first in the aisle. She gave me a firm and friendly handsake, a gracious smile, then turned and jostled down the aisle. She'd get a copy of *From My Window* -- and I'd write her story for my book.

When I got home and warmed up my expensive Toshiba 1100 + and looked for the little note Theresa Griffin had written, it just wasn't there. I've had many frustrations as I've struggled with these damn computers, but this one tops them all. I know now what's happened; I've done it all before. I forgot to press the SAVE button before I put the damn thing away. So she'll never see this story unless she writes to me.

Theresa Griffin is the girl I forgot to save.

BOSTON'S CANAGHAN TUNNEL

I was on the Massachusetts Parkway, headed for Boston and Salem State for my first Elderhostel. I was driving a rented Lynx, and fighting my way through a heavy downpour. I really should stop and wait for better weather, but I pounded on. What drove me? Or was I being led?

Two years ago I'd followed a hunch and driven through a rainstorm, just like this. The storm had chased me from Buffalo to Fonda N.Y., and the next day I found the parents of Andrew Kimmerly.

I ducked into Howard Johnson's, got a large coffee-to-go, laced it with cream and sugar, and pushed on to Boston.

The freeway tried to ease us over the Appalachian mountains. The rain thickened as we scraped the bottom of the clouds. The traffic slowed. The visibility dropped to 200 feet. I got an eerie feeling I was being held back. I checked the doors and windows expecting them to spout water. We passed the summit but not the fury of the storm.

The eastern sky brightened for a moment only to refresh the down-pour. "Miles to Boston" grew smaller. Another lane was added to the freeway. The rain lessened to a dismal drizzle. Traffic thickened and dreary rows of rain-soaked houses fringed the road.

The freeway squeezed between warehouses and railway tracks. Green water-logged direction signs grew more numerous and more confusing. I saw the sky-scrapered outline of downtown Boston, and knew I was fast approaching mile zero.

The woman at the information centre had warned me not to go through Boston, but cousin Will Smart said it was the best route to take on a Sunday. Boston's circle and a mile-long tunnel under the harbour would lead me to 1A and Salem State.

"End of Freeway", the sooty green sign warned.

164

Keep to the right, Gordon, and follow 1A.

Suddenly I had three choices. Saw two 1A signs. Braked. Got tooted at and scooted to the right.

"To Tunnels", said the sign. I was in the circle, tunnel hunting. Three lanes became two and I saw the sign, "Canaghan Tunnel".

I became the hunted. Somehow I'd lost the outside lane. I was on the inside lane and the sign screamed, "TUNNEL TRAFFIC RIGHT 2 LANES". I swung over. Horns blared. I thought a pickup truck would tear off my right fender, while a Beetle Bug tried to mount me from the rear.

Two lanes held three cars. They juggled forward like a herd of range cattle crowding through a chute. I inched along waiting for the crunch of metal. Towering walls of glass and concrete threatened. If the stampede of cars didn't get me, a skyscraper would. I couldn't escape. I'd ride through. I had to.

The two lanes narrowed to one. Scowling drivers lipped curses as they jockeyed forward. Finally the tunnel arched into view. "FORM 2 LINES", said the sign. How the hell can you make two lines out of the six rows of metal-charging steers?

My Lynx squeezed to her smallest size. Bared her claws. We got braver. Nudged a bumper. Threatened to claw a gleaming Caddy, and then crowded into the tunnel's hole.

The overhead yellow sodium lights spooked the sweating tunnel walls. Red tail-lights bloodied the greasy pavement. Brake lights screamed against the arched ceiling. Some silly bastards fought for position as turn-signals spread orange and red flames along the tunnel walls. A truck's motor backfired beside me. *My god! I've been shot, and in this hell hole!*

I checked the windows, afraid the gooey moisture oozing from the walls and ceiling might splash into the car. The charging vehicles drove like crazed escapees afraid the tunnel would never end, changing lanes in their mad rush to find the exit.

Daylight softened the spooky yellow. The end couldn't be far. A lumbering truck slowed, hazard lights flashing as it struggled out of the yellow hell. The car behind cut around me and the truck. I asked the Lynx to follow, and she did, pulling me from the hell-hole to the brightness of a dull New England sky, and we slipped out under the sign "1A North", and ran like a scared rabbit to search for Salem State.

AMERICAN EFFICIENCY

I have always admired the ability of our American neighbours to get things done.

In January of 1942, with Pearl Harbour only six weeks old, the American invasion of Edmonton began. With the Japanese threatening America, the sea-lanes to Alaska were vulnerable — the American navy couldn't protect them. Alaska would have to be supplied by land. A road would have to be built through the Canadian/Alaskan far northern wilderness.

"We'll build the damn road!" hollered the Americans, over the roar of their bulldozers.

We Canadians didn't have a decent highway across our country -- and here was Uncle Sam going to build a road to Alaska! With all 1877 miles protected by muskeg, mountains and mosquitoes.

"The war will be over before they get halfway to Fairbanks," we sneered.

But it wasn't. Six months later, in July of 1942, the first convoy of dusty, mud-covered trucks crawled into Fairbanks...

As airmen, we Canadians saw the same efficiency in Africa. We'd survived nine months of powdered eggs, bread-sausages and ersatz coffee in rationed-ravaged England. Now we were on our way to India. But our four-engine Lancaster bomber with its Merlin engines couldn't land or take off in the sweltering heat of the Sahara Desert. We'd have to fly at night.

We spent the first day at the Royal Air Force (RAF) Bengazhi base, in Tripoli (where Montgomery whipped Rommel). The temperature rose to 115 degrees. The sun blistered our anemic British tans, and the desert wind whipped sand into eyes, nose and mouth and even into the stewed dates served with every meal. The canteen sold warm beer. Or for tuppence you could buy a glass of lukewarm water — stored in a goatskin, with one leg used as a spigot.

As daylight and the heat left the desert, our Lancaster left the runway. We'd fly to Cairo for tomorrow's heat...

The emerging day greyed the eastern sky. The lights of Cairo rolled reassuringly over the horizon. Dawn jewelled the turquoise of the Nile and sparkled her emerald borders as she meandered to the pyramids.

"We'll land at the American Base," blared the intercom. "Bloody RAF still haven't fixed the holes Rommel left in their runways."

"You guys must be hungry," the American duty-sergeant said, when our pilot had parked the Lanc and signed us in. "There's a restaurant in the far hangar. Opens at six. They serve great bacon and eggs."

"A restaurant? You've got a real restaurant — with bacon and eggs?"

Forty-five years later I still marvel at that bit of Americana, spic-and-span in the dusty Sahara. Hear the bacon sizzling. Smell the toast and coffee. Taste those fried eggs and hash-browns. I'll remember that Cairo breakfast till the day I die.

Two years ago I registered at Mesa Community College (MCC) in Arizona. The desert-flat campus, with its low flat-topped buildings sprawling behind acres of herringboned parking lots, squats in the middle of downtown Mesa. I felt out of place among all those youngsters. I kept looking for the gray hair and wrinkles of Venture Out people, like myself.

But these kids helped me, and in less than half an hour I was enrolled in MCC. That same old American efficiency.

Today I'm back again. There aren't as many students, but they've added red arrows, direction signs and an information kiosk for briefing. It looks simple, efficient and American... except they've added computers.

I have to get past three of them. One is hidden in the cafeteria. Another guards the Registrar's office. The third (where they take your money), has an armed policeman on duty. It takes me three visits to each computer to satisfy the data-gobbling little monsters. The first machine, with its finger-flying operator, says—because I'm a foreign student -- I must have a visa number.

"I'm a Canadian. I don't need a visa to come into your country."

"I'm sorry, sir, but the computer won't accept your registration without a visa number."

"I registered two years ago. See if I'm in the machine," and I give her my name.

I'm there, all right. But it takes two more tries, and an okay from the programmer to convince the young woman. However, nothing can convince the computer. "Just hit the over-ride key," says the programmer. She does. The cursor winks. My name and address flash on the screen.

The second machine wants my age, sex, birthplace, my wife's name, religion ... "and your social security number?" asks the operator.

"721-701-421".

The computer beeps and flashes. "Error entry not compatible," warns the screen. I brace myself for another battle, and dig out my social insurance card.

"Let's try '721-70-1421' ... yes, it's okay," and she smiles. "You'll find the bursar in room LA 6, just follow the arrows." I pass the guarded door, cheque book in hand, and brave the last computer.

More beeps and flashing lights. "You're taking the same course twice."

"That's right, I'm taking the evening and afternoon in Creative Writing."

"Nobody's ever done that before. The computer won't accept it. You'll have to delete one of the classes and have it initialed by your counsellor."

I find the counsellor. Get her initials. Pass the policeman for the second time. Face the blinking green-faced little monster.

"Sorry sir, the class is filled."

"Filled? It wasn't filled when I saw my counsellor two hours ago!"

"I can't overload the class without the approval of the head of the English faculty."

Twenty minutes and a mile later I pass the armed guard for the third time. "Good luck," he smiles, and I need it — it's taken three hours and three miles of concrete to enroll in MCC Creative Writing.

I still admire the way Americans get things done. But be careful, neighbour — or those beeping machines with their blinking screens may wreck your reputation.

DEBRA

Los Angeles' Orange County airport hummed with organized confusion. Thanksgiving week-enders jammed the ticket counters. I was next in line, headed for Air California's check-in when she plunked her bags at my feet, "Sorry miss, but this is the front of the line."

She had entered the boarding area with the easy grace of a well- seasoned traveler. Beige rugby pants with a matching jacket over a baby blue sweater gave a soft college chicness to her peach complexion. A soft fuzziness neatly ruled her blonde hair. Low bangs and large-lensed glasses tried to hide smiling blue eyes. Blue plastic slippers covered her sockless feet. She carried the independent air of a college senior.

"Is this the line for Air Cal?" she asked.

"Yes," I replied. She started to drag two well-traveled duffle bags, an overstuffed boarding bag, a satchel-like purse and a tennis racket. "You might as well leave your bags here, it's not that far to the end of the line."

"Thanks", she smiled.

Bodies milled about the boarding area, and there was standing room only; most of the flights were running late. Air Cal's flight to San Francisco and Vancouver was already late with no plane on the ramp. I gazed over the chattering herd, amazed at the ant hill of activity. Where were they going? Would they get there? What would they find? Why were they going? I studied their faces. Then I spotted her again.

She found a couple of vacant square feet next to the wall, dropped her bag on the floor, nestled herself cross-legged on the bag and pulled a book from her purse. An envelope fell from the book. She grabbed it from the floor and gently kissed it. Tears escaped from behind the large-lensed glasses. A warm smile glowed as she read the letter and tenderly tucked it into her purse.

Air Cal flight 914 was called and I found my right-hand non-smoking window seat. I seat-buckled myself and watched my fellow travelers find their seats, wondering who I'd have for a companion. "Is this 7C?" I heard someone ask. I looked up and there was my letter friend.

"I'm in 7E, that's 7C on the aisle." I watched her wrestle her pregnant flight bag and her tennis racket into the overhead luggage rack.

She smiled as she buckled her seat belt and said, "You look like a Canadian; you must be going to Vancouver."

"That's right. Where are you going?"

"Home to Vancouver Island. Do you know where Courtenay is?"

"Excuse me, are you Debra Rogers?" It was the stewardess.

"Yes I am."

"Here's a message for you," and she handed her a note.

"Oh my God!" she cried. "I gotta get off this plane!" With a mad scramble she gathered her bag, her purse and tennis racket and rushed to the exit. I watched as she tumbled down the gangway and ran into the arms of a young man. My eyes dropped to the seat. I picked up the note written in large felt pen letters. I read, "I'M SORRY PLEASE COME BACK. I LOVE YOU. JIM."

Guess I never will find the connection between Debra Rogers and my home town.

From My Window

Poems

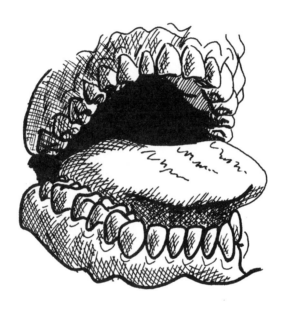

NEW TEETH

Damn the pain it hurts like hell
As I await the Christmas break
Must I give up my season's take
Without my teeth to help me make
My weight go up my belly bulge

One doc says I'll lose them all
Doc Gunnel lays it on the line
With five lose three save two
And build anew add one to help

He yanks and pulls
He digs and drills

I live with toothless smile
He presses wax and builds a plate
It's light and firm and hurts a bit
He adjusts it here and there

I sink my new-found teeth
Into an apple hard they bite I chew
They're really great and as I await
To test them on my first tough steak
I give my thanks to the Greenfield crew
For an appetite they help renew.

January 1985

HOMOCHRONOS

WHAT GREG HILL'S STATUE MEANT TO ME *

Is this me?

Has my life been put upon a pole
Atop a curved stick for all to see?
Must I rest forever as a question mark
With furrowed brow and hopeless face?
Can I not change fickle fate
Enjoy the peace that death may bring?

Place me not in the shades of doubt
As I await the answers of eternity:
Let my ashes go to dust from whence I came,
To float among the stars
Seeking love and loved ones.

Strike down the cursed question mark.
Let me find the peace that earth denied,
Renew my love for all mankind
And save some for myself.

February 1985

* Gabriele Rico, *Writing the Natural Way*
(J.P. Tracher, Inc. Los Angeles, 1983), page 184.

Shirley Wagner

SHIRLEY WAGNER 1945 - 1973

I'm terminal
I know I'm going to die
Who says that now's the time?
I'll fight. I'll show those quacks
Just stop this pain and let me heal.
I don't fear the future
Nor regret the distant past.
Just let me live today
Despite the aches and pains.
Let me see my loved ones;
Let me hear their voices ring;
Let me feel their childish softness.
Bring them in beyond the door.
I'll flee this room of whiteness,
Escape the nagging of despair.
People come to comfort,
Some with gifts and prayers.
Bring me the sound of beaches,
The hush of an autumn sunset
From across a quiet bay.
Bring me the smiles of children.
I'll take them all with me.

Bring me the strength
For my unchartered journey.
I'll be leaving soon you know.
Your love will ease the parting
When peace replaces pain.

March 1985

Keith Wagner

KEITH

This is a poem to my son, Keith
Born in adversity, the first of four
Fragile, yet strong you conquered all.
You grew up too fast for a sensitive child.
Pushed you at school so you'd be like me
Failed to see the man in your soul.
Good with your brain and good with your hands.
The emotions I felt from your photos and art
Their beauty still lies close to my heart.
You met your problems head on,
Your marriage, your home and retarded Leona,
Kathie, your substitute for a son,
You spoiled rotten, but Kathie survived.
Cancer struck and you bravely fought back
Charged into surveying no challenge too great.
You needed my love and got caught in my drive.
Seven years of treatment helped you survive.
Three times they tore your festers apart,
You struggled back for another fresh start.
You surrendered your eye but never gave up.
I watched you die and I tried to help.
I wrote of my love, unwound my heart.
I wondered why I'd left it so late,
For thirty-six years is too long to wait.
The wounds of grief are a smoothed-over scar.
While you could be a meandering star.
You're still thirty-six; I'm twice that now.
I'll be joining you soon, wherever you are
You'll be easy to find.

18 February 1985

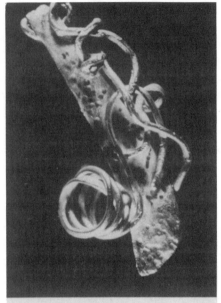

gure 9–4   GLENDA BOGEN, *UNTITLED*, COURTESY OF THE SCULPTOR.

WHAT GLENDA BOGEN'S SCULPTURE
MEANT TO ME

A frog, glued to lily pad, sits like some absent-minded professor at the traffic light waiting for an unwary fly to run a red light. His telescopic eyes, perched above his head of green hair, rotates as his radar scans the air traffic buzzing above the swamp. Eel grass snakes up between the lily pads, and coils around the frog's jumping legs. He is anchored to the mucky bottom of his swamp. A dragon fly helicopters above the lily pads. The frog's radar measures the closing distance. The biplane insect enters the killing range of the camouflaged hunter. The frog strikes like green lightning. A splash and plunk, the eel grass holds and jerks the frog. The dragon fly escapes. The floundering frog disappears into the jaws of a cruising pike. . . .

The end

* Rico, page 195.

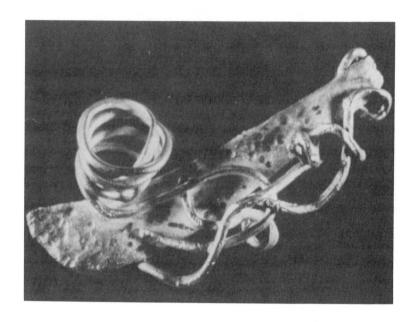

WHAT GLENDA BOGEN'S SCULPTURE
MEANT TO ME UPSIDE DOWN *

My God! It's my inner ear. Lying in my hand like a fresh-cooked shrimp, all fleshy-pink and embryo-like, and with my hearing aid attached. The hearing aid dangles from my hand like a broken hair-spring from some giant's pocket watch. The hearing aid squeals in protest, and I try to hush and hide the unsightly mess as I approach Venture Out's security gate. I close my hand. I feel a wiggling in my fist. I peek once as I break the sheet of paper strung across the guarded gate. My fist has become a squirming stump, a battlefield for crawling worms and bugs ...

I awake to find Rico's *Writing the Natural Way* spread across my sleepy face.

* Rico, page 195.

Edith Carwithen

AN ODE TO A SECRETARY

The note said, "Edith Carwithen's dead."
It can't be true, there must be some mistake.
How can my efficient secretary be no more?
No more notes, no files to find.
She's gone? You're sure? She won't be back?
She left my office years ago but not my mind,
Nor I her's, since I'd phone to ask if she recalled

An ancient file or some weathered survey plan.
To those who'll miss her more than I,
Whose hearts and souls are racked with pain:
Watch for her in the evening sky,
Amongst the sparkling eyes of night.
Her star will be alive and bright.
Take its light into your soul, and hold it tight.
It will help to heal the wounds
And to seek her out when you depart.

March 1987

From My Window

Jimmy Barry

JIMMY BARRY   1974 - 1986

You're too young for your new journey
We know you'll find your way
We hope to guide and help you
With love by night and day.

You're too young to wander
In vast spaces of eternity
In the starlit skies of night
We'll see you passing by.

You're too young to miss the living
That aged life can bring
You'll find the joy of loving
As your roam from star to star.

You're not too young to feel the heartache
As we put your things away
Our souls will glow with memories
Our wounds of grief to heal.

May 1986

Lloyd Edwards

LLOYD EDWARDS 1913 - 1987

Lloyd left us in an awful hurry,
Forgot to leave his calling card
To say when he'd be back.
I'll miss his infectious chuckle
And his wide-faced grin
Beaming from atop his six-four tower,
And shaded with his favorite cowboy hat.
The shock of his departure stirred memories:
Of prairie towns and Edward's farm,
Of Markinch Scouts and Tuxis Boys,
Of baseball games and tennis courts,
And old Ford cars that wouldn't go.
To those whose memories outnumber mine,
Whose hearts and souls are wrenched with grief,
Watch for him in the evening sky,
Amongst the sparkling eyes of night.
His star will be alive and bright;
Take its light into your soul, and hold it tight.
It will help to heal the wounds
And seek him out when you depart.

March 1986

From My Window

V.O. SPRING

Does April bring to Venture Out
A waning and a waxing?
Do silver-shaded windows, deserted streets
And empty lots bid fare-thee-well?
Some heed the call of black Ohioan soil.
Others flee the desert's dusty heat
To chill in the coastal forest rain.
Some seek out the prairie plain
For luscious greens of growing grain.
Others break hibernating shells
With plans to visit every state.
Strange creatures we migrating folk
As in our so-called golden years
We seek the best of many worlds.
Shorter days and shivery nights
Will lead us back to Venture Out
To winter there and play about.

April 1985

From My Window

LET US LIVE

I'll never live long enough
To lower the water in the well of knowledge
To open a book and not find
A new way to express an old idea.
I'll never live long enough
To exhaust the beauty of a sunrise
To melt the glory of a prairie sunset
To shy at the grace of a beautiful woman.

I'll never live long enough
Not to thrill to the touch of softness
Stored in the magic of delicate skin
The lustre of pearls the sheen of silver.
I'll never live long enough
To tire of the taste of fine wine
The nip of aged cheese
The tongue-tingle of champagne.
I'll never live long enough
Not to cherish the song of a thrush
The strings of Strauss a cricket's chirp
Or an eagle's swish.

I'll never live long enough
Just to die but I'll enrich my soul
With an earthy smell a rainbow's arch
The touch of silk and the taste of tea.
I'll never live long enough
But I will live

February 1985

TIME

time fascinates punctuates eliminates
time soothes eludes and pursues
time's limited unlimited and endless
seconds gone never return
there's much to do it's ever so late
the world spins time no brakes no reverse
What would you do if time stood still
give your love to those unloved
grab the bargains hindsight sees
too late too late cries fumbling faith
it's never too late to begin again
to heal the wounds to love anew
tick tock counts the terror of time
heed the sound ere your days are gone
pause to think of the love untold
awake and live in the here-and-now
it may be your last chance
this time around

March 1987

Sam Skinner

ODE TO SAM SKINNER

Sam's slipped the fettered bounds of earth,
Freed himself from pain and strife.
Escaped the fog of his uncharted journey
To fly in the limitless skies of eternity,
Seeking among the countless stars
Strength and peace that earth denied.
Free to fly beyond the sun
Free to find loved ones gone,
Free to wait for loves to come.
In the darkened skies of night
You'll see Sam's star alive and bright.
Mark it well for its pure light
Will heal the recent wounds of grief.
Sam Skinner's star will give us strength
To find our way when we depart.

December 1985

Sam, a pilot in the R.C.A.F., died of cancer at age 57.

From My Window

COMOX BAY'S OCTOBER

It's Sunday morning and we're back on Standard Time. I'm sitting at our kitchen counter, set in a window over-looking the calm waters of Comox Bay. The soft glow of a new day enhances the flavor of the butter-soaked toast, the garden-fresh tomatoes, and the eggs I gathered yesterday. I linger over the last of my coffee, breathing in the beauty of our bay.

My eyes follow the moss-covered rail fence as it zigzags across the lawn to the beach. The gray-blue waters of the high tide lap lazily against the green edge of the lawn. Last night's storm has left a pile of leaves neatly nestled against the fence. Ducks and seagulls rest sleepily amongst the bobbing flotsam.

From My Window

I search the skyline for the mountain tops, but they are lost, shrouded in mist and low clouds. A small thunderstorm hides a valley, while ropes of rain anchor low cloud to the green forest. I scan the mountain sides trying to peer under the hood of the gray clouds, then follow the shoreline as it holds the mountains in place. Despite the dull light, autumn colours sprinkle the rain forest with patches of yellow, red and gold.

Now from across the bay the scattered houses of Royston emerge, one by one, from the misty camouflage. People live there. I'm not alone with the ducks and the seagulls.

Evening is here. Curdled clouds blanket the bay; the sun hidden behind the mountains, but still alive, shines delicate cranberry to tint the baby clouds; the mountain tops scallop a silhouette against the fading sky; a smooth, steel-gray mirror covers the bay and reflects the twinkling lights of Royston. The sky darkens and Venus, bright and just above the mountains, bids the day goodbye.

Ivy Wagner

The Author

Gordon Wagner was born and raised in Markinch Saskatchewan. A graduate of the University of Saskatchewan, he worked two years underground in Sudbury's nickel mines and then he spent five years in the Royal Canadian Airforce, logging time in twenty one countries. He settled in Courtenay after World War II, obtained a commission as British Columbia Land Surveyor and later qualified as Notary Public.

He retired seven years ago and cleared twenty acres of swamp for his ranch, the Flying W. He raised Simmental cattle, buying high and selling low. He unloaded the farm two years ago.

Four years ago he went back to school to learn to write. *From My Window* takes you over the trails he has travelled in his seventy-three years.

Gordon Wagner

203

From My Window